Dialogues on Revelation
with
John the Apostle

What would the apostle John say about
Jesus and our times in light of the
Revelation?

Yann Opsitch

Keledei
PUBLICATIONS

An Imprint of Sulis International Press
Los Angeles | Dallas | London

Cover photo: *San Giovanni Evangelista a Patmos* (*John the Apostle on Patmos*) by Jacopo Vignali (17th century). Photo by Giovanni Piccirillo (a cura di), La chiesa dei Santi Michele e Gaetano, Becocci Editore, Firenze 2006.

Unless indicated otherwise, Scripture quotations are from the English Standard Version (ESV) Copyright © 2001 by Crossway, Good News Publishers.

ISBN (print): 978-1-958139-04-2
ISBN (eBook): 978-1-958139-05-9

Published by Keledei Publications
An Imprint of Sulis International
Los Angeles | Dallas | London

www.sulisinternational.com

To my children, their spouses and to my grandchildren.

Contents

QUESTIONS TO JOHN

This book presents a fictional dialogue with the apostle John. Is it possible to know what John might have answered to a number of our questions about the book of Revelation? Yes, it is possible to a large extent since we have his Gospel, three of his epistles and the Old and New Testaments. As we ask questions to John, would we always receive the answers we hope for or expect? Are there more answers or different answers we may wish the Lord would give us? I don't doubt that this will often be the case.

Revelation does not contradict what we learn from the Gospels or epistles of the New Testament; it is not some kind of new "gospel" and does not offer a different teaching from everything else in Scripture (see Paul's warning in Galatians 1.6-9).

Genesis 3.15 refers to the essential battle between the posterity of the woman and the posterity of the serpent, in other words the spiritual battle between human beings and Satan, God's adversary. This battle is found throughout Scripture, but forms an essential background to the book of Revelation from

1

the first to the last chapter. Revelation reminds us of what Paul wrote in his letter to the Christians in Ephesus about their struggle with Satan:

> "Finally, be strong in the Lord and in the strength of his might. **11** Put on the whole armor of God, that you may be able to stand against the schemes of the devil. **12** For we do not wrestle against flesh and blood, but against the rulers, against the authorities, against the cosmic powers over this present darkness, against the spiritual forces of evil in the heavenly places. **13** Therefore take up the whole armor of God, that you may be able to withstand in the evil day, and having done all, to stand firm." (Ephesians 6.10-13).

The book of Revelation helps us see things from the perspective of eternity, of heaven. The heavenly perspective shown to John is one that is full of expectation and hope. However, the earthly perspective is one of pain and struggle. John himself is exiled on Patmos and writes to the churches in Asia as their "partner in the tribulation and the kingdom and the patient endurance that are in Jesus, was on the island called Patmos because of the word of God and the testimony of Jesus." (1.9).

The tribulations these early Christians were enduring are directly connected to "the word of God" and "the testimony of Jesus". It was the preaching and teaching of the early Church that provoked the strong opposition of first century Roman culture. The word of God acted like a "sword" into the heart and life of the Roman pagan culture (see Hebrews 4.12) bringing some back to God through faith and repentance but also bringing others to reject these words contrary to everything they had grown up with, especially the significance of the gods they had grown up worshipping.

15"From his mouth comes a sharp sword with which to strike down the nations, and he will rule them with a rod of iron. He will tread the winepress of the fury of the wrath of God the Almighty. **16** On his robe and on his thigh, he has a name written, King of kings and Lord of lords." (19.15,16)

My prayer is that this reading will be a blessing to those who will return to Revelation with a renewed interest: "Blessed is the one who reads aloud the words of this prophecy, and blessed are those who hear, and who keep what is written in it, for the time is near." (Revelation 1.3).

1. MY LORD IS RISEN

"**17** When I saw him, I fell at his feet as though dead.
But he laid his right hand on me, saying, 'Fear not, I
am the first and the last, **18** and the living one. I died,
and behold I am alive forevermore, and I have the keys
of Death and Hades.'" (Revelation 1.17,18)

*

On the island of Patmos and on the first day of the week, the
resurrected Lord appeared to me in glory and spoke to me,
commanding me to write all that I would see and hear.

I have been exiled on Patmos for over three years. My exile
happened shortly before emperor Nero committed suicide,
bringing an end to the rule of the Julio-Claudians over Rome
and the Empire. At the time of my exile on Patmos, the Romans were at war with our people in the land of Israel. The
rulers and even inhabitants of the Empire do not really understand the differences between Jews and Christians. My exile is

part of this anti-Jewish policy that started under Claudius and has continued.

From the only hill of Patmos and watching over the bleak Aegean Sea, I have spent many days in great loneliness — a loneliness growing deeper in my heart when the weather was clement and the sun shining, when I could distinguish the coast of Anatolia about sixty-five millum passa away.

I have been able to have food delivered to me and even a few letters thanks to the devotion of our brethren. But this is not always possible, and often I feel great hunger. But the greatest hunger has been the hunger in my heart to see and hear again my resurrected Lord.

I have learned that the world is now under the power of a new ruler by the name of Vespasian, who conquered Rome after the civil wars following Nero's death. Vespasian is one of the heads of the beast from the sea shown to me in the Revelation.

I have also read through letters from the brethren that life under Vespasian is not so harsh for the disciples in Rome. However, I also know the brutality and pagan ways of the local leaders in Ephesus and the other cities of Anatolia and beyond, even to the ends of the vast empire built by Rome.

In his book of Acts, written after his Gospel, our brother Luke recalls the travels of Paul and how many came to the faith in Ephesus; how others burned their books of magic arts and how the word of the Lord increased in that city. Luke also tells us how Demetrius of Ephesus, who made and sold shrines of the goddess Artemis, attempted to have Paul and his co-workers arrested and beaten.

All the cities of the Empire are full of idols and especially patron gods and goddesses. These deities are seen as special protectors of cities and different trades in these cities and regions. Not worshipping or honoring these patron gods produces outrage and violence on the part of the local populations against the Church everywhere. Thus, the disciples of the Lord are nowhere able to live at peace and without threats to their lives and families.

When the Lord appeared in glory on that day, the first day of the week, it had been over thirty years since our Lord Jesus had been crucified and rose from the dead after three days in the tomb of Joseph of Arimathea. I did not know if I would ever see him or hear his voice again in my life on this earth. The last time I heard his voice, when I was still a young man, it was at his ascension after spending forty days with us his apostles in teaching and beautiful fellowship. He had just been telling us that we would be his witnesses in Jerusalem, in all of Judea and Samaria and to the end of the earth. He was suddenly lifted up, a cloud taking him out of our sight.

On other occasions, he later appeared in his glorious resurrected body, once to five hundred brethren at once. He also appeared to the persecutor of the Church, Saul, on the road to Damascus. Saul was called Paul by our Lord and made by him his apostle to the gentiles.

After preaching and teaching with Peter and other apostles in Judea, we all were scattered throughout the nations of the earth to bear witness to our Lord. On the cross, Jesus had given me the care of his mother. After years of service in Judea and the land of Israel, Mary and I came to Ephesus to minister to the large and growing body of believers in that city. After many years of service to the Church in Ephesus, opposition grew against those who preached and taught the brethren.

When the Lord appeared in glory on that first day of the week, the joy of seeing him in his glory and hearing his loving voice filled my heart. I overcame the sense of loneliness living alone in exile, and I completely recovered my hope. I knew that the Lord was completely in charge of all the events of my life, the events in the life of His Church and the events of the world.

"Surely, I am coming soon." These last words of my Lord in the Revelation are now engravened upon my heart, never to be forgotten". Amen. Come, Lord Jesus.

2. THE REVELATION OF JESUS CHRIST

"**1** The revelation of Jesus Christ, which God gave him to show to his servants the things that must soon take place. He made it known by sending his angel to his servant John, **2** who bore witness to the word of God and to the testimony of Jesus Christ, even to all that he saw." (Revelation 1.1,2)

*

John, the Revelation has been given to God's people over two thousand years ago. Many generations have passed from this life and the world is still a place where we so often find hatred instead of love, unrighteousness instead of righteousness. It is often the case that believers become discouraged. This Revelation was given to you on Patmos and for the entire Church of our Lord as a word of comfort. Many today are still preaching or teaching from the Revelation to encourage their brethren.

But some are doing so in ways that bring about confusion and doubt.

Tell me a little more about that. What is being preached from the Revelation in this distant future you talk about?

A lot of this preaching we hear today focuses on the disasters and calamities described in the Revelation, such as plagues or wars. This preaching is used by many to convince people that we are at the time of Christ's return, that these great tragedies are signs of his coming soon for judgment and the resurrection of the dead.

Well, Yann it is clear that the Lord will return in glory to judge the world and for the resurrection of the dead, "when he comes on that day to be glorified in his saints and to be marveled at among all who have believed" as the apostle Paul wrote to the brethren in Thessalonica. (2 Thessalonians 1.10). There would be no comfort and no hope from any portion of the Scriptures if that were not the case.

What I mean is that there is a lot of preaching today especially from the Revelation concerning signs that would show the Lord soon returning in his glory. Is the message of the Revelation about the "last days", the time preceding the return of our Lord?

Are you living in the last days? Yes, unless the Lord has already returned. Not only that but myself here in Patmos and all our brethren in the world today are living in the last days.

But are not the "last days" in the Scriptures those times when the Lord returns in glory?

In the Scriptures the last days are the times that extend from the incarnation of our Lord until his return in glory, not the immediate time that precedes his return. Thus, the writer to the Hebrews for example writes that "in these last days" God has spoken to us by his son, whom he appointed the heir of all things. (Hebrews 1.1). Today as I live in exile on Patmos and as our Lord is warning us of terrible persecutions coming upon the Church, we are in the last days. Our brother Peter preaching on Pentecost declared that the signs that occurred on that day and the speaking in foreign tongues were in "the last days" as prophesied by the prophet Joel. (Acts 2.14-21). And the "last days" will extend in time until our Lord returns in glory.

Many today do not understand how the Revelation can be helpful to them, especially if it is describing great times of persecution of the early Church.

The Scriptures, for the most part, are teaching us about the actions and teachings from God in the past and which are a source of comfort for all generations. However, as our brother Paul wrote to the brothers and sisters in Rome, "Whatever was written in former days was written for our instruction, that through endurance and through the encouragement of the Scriptures we might have hope" (Romans 15.4)

But suppose that the Revelation was written mostly about events in the future how would it be a source of encouragement for us, for our churches today in this terrible persecution we are about to endure? The Revelation given to us today will one day become a word of God concerning the past, but this is the case with most of the Scriptures which are still a great source of encouragement and hope.

Is some of the misunderstanding about Revelation not due to the fact that over two thousand years have passed, and the Lord has not returned yet?

This would not be surprising. Even today while I am exiled on Patmos there are those who are teaching that the Lord has already come or will return soon in his glory. This was the case not too long ago with some teachers among the brethren in Thessalonica. The apostle Paul needed to warn these brethren and teachers that such teaching was not in agreement with God's revealed will. Writing to the Church in Thessalonica, Paul mentions the resurrection of the dead and how those still alive being caught up together with the resurrected saints to meet the Lord. However, the apostle at once warns these brethren not to speculate about "the times and seasons" when these events would occur. He explains this with the image of the thief who comes in the night, unannounced to rob people, when they least expect him:

> "**5** Now concerning the times and the seasons, broth-
> ers, you have no need to have anything written to
> you. **2** For you yourselves are fully aware that the day
> of the Lord will come like a thief in the night. **3** While
> people are saying, 'There is peace and security'
> then sudden destruction will come upon them as labor
> pains come upon a pregnant woman, and they will not
> escape. **4** But you are not in darkness, brothers, for that
> day to surprise you like a thief. **5** For you are all chil-
> dren of light, children of the day. We are not of the
> night or of the darkness. **6** So then let us not sleep, as
> others do, but let us keep awake and be sober." (1
> Thessalonians 5.1-4).

In his second letter to these brethren our brother Paul warned them about teachers claiming the Lord had already returned,

> "**2** Now concerning the coming of our Lord Jesus
> Christ and our being gathered together to him, we ask
> you, brothers, **2** not to be quickly shaken in mind
> or alarmed, either by a spirit or a spoken word, or a

letter seeming to be from us, to the effect that the day of the Lord has come." (2 Thessalonians 2.1,2).

In the same letter our brother Paul exhorts these brethren to "stand firm and hold firm to the traditions that you were taught by us, either by our spoken word or by our letter" (2 Thessalonians 2.15).

Did not the apostle Peter also respond to those who were impatient about the Lord's return and wanted to know about the exact time of his return?

Peter teaches that some will mock the faith saying "Where is the promise of his coming? For ever since the fathers fell asleep, all things are continuing as they were from the beginning of creation?" (2 Peter 3.3).

Peter warned these mockers reminding them of the truth already found in our Psalms:

> **"1** Lord, you have been our dwelling place
>   in all generations.
> **2** Before the mountains were brought forth,
>   or ever you had formed the earth and the world,
>   from everlasting to everlasting you are God.
> **3** You return man to dust
>   and say, "Return, O children of man!"
> **4** For a thousand years in your sight
>   are but as yesterday when it is past,
>   or as a watch in the night." (Psalm 90.1-4; 2 Peter 3.8).

I now remember that the great lesson the Lord conveys to us is that with Him "one day is as a thousand years, and a thousand years as one day". God's timing and our timing are different!

God does not always reveal to us everything we would like to know.

Remember also how our brother Peter preached on the first Pentecost as recorded by Luke, saying that the Lord was received into heaven "until the time for restoring all the things about which God spoke by the mouth of his holy prophets long ago" (Acts 3.21). This was mentioned for example by Isaiah the prophet. (Isaiah 65.17; 66.22).

Is the time of restoring all things spoken by the prophets still future?

The letter to the Hebrews reminds us that the Creator has a plan to renew all things in his creation as well as the life of the faithful, as already taught in the Psalms:

> **10**"You, Lord, laid the foundation of the earth in the beginning,
>   and the heavens are the work of your hands;
> **11** they will perish, but you remain;
>   they will all wear out like a garment,
> **12** like a robe you will roll them up,
>   like a garment they will be changed.
> But you are the same, and your years will have no
> end." (Hebrews 1.11,12; Psalms 102. 25-27).

All of this has to do with the Lord's return in glory!

Yes, and at the same time we need to understand that we are already partakers of these promises. The Kingdom of God's Son is the glorious Kingdom of which David's rule was only a vague shadow. In Christ we have been introduced into this kingdom of light and perfect joy and peace. The Lord has already brought about a "new creation" through those who have come to him and have already been raised with him to a new life. (Colossians 2.8-3.11). Those who have been born anew, born from above, who have been born "of water and the Spirit" are in the Lord's eyes "a new creation":

> "**16** From now on, therefore, we regard no one according to the flesh. Even though we once regarded Christ according to the flesh, we regard him thus no longer. **17** Therefore, if anyone is in Christ, he is a new creation. The old has passed away; behold, the new has come. **18** All this is from God, who through Christ reconciled us to himself and gave us the ministry of reconciliation;" (2 Corinthians 5.16-18; John 3.1-7)

Did not the apostle Paul write that our brothers and sisters in the Lord have already been raised with him because of their faith, in the waters of baptism?

The wonderful truth about our baptism in the name of our Lord is that it is stamped with God's promise of forgiveness, the gift of his Holy Spirit and eternal life, as preached by Peter on the day of Pentecost. (Acts 2.37-41). Our brother Paul confirms this preaching of Peter in a number of his letters, as in his letters to Rome or Colossae. (Romans 6.1-4; Colossians 2.6-15)

Does the Revelation also not teach about a resurrection found in this life through our faith in the Lord?

Yes, it does. And it is one of the central truths of the Revelation from the Lord Jesus the Christ.

The believer has already passed from death to life, from darkness to light through the work of our Lord Jesus as well as faith in him and repentance. The new life in Christ is a present reality but is also full of promises for the future; we should not separate those two as the apostle Peter preached in the temple before being arrested by the priests and Sadducees:

17 "And now, brothers, I know that you acted in ignorance, as did also your rulers. **18** But what God fore-
told by the mouth of all the prophets, that his Christ
would suffer, he thus fulfilled. **19** Repent therefore,
and turn back, that your sins may be blotted
out, **20** that times of refreshing may come from the
presence of the Lord, and that he may send the
Christ appointed for you, Jesus, **21** whom heaven must
receive until the time for restoring all the things about
which God spoke by the mouth of his holy prophets
long ago. **22** Moses said, 'The Lord God will raise up
for you a prophet like me from your brothers. You shall
listen to him in whatever he tells you. **23** And it shall
be that every soul who does not listen to that
prophet shall be destroyed from the people.' **24** And all
the prophets who have spoken, from Samuel and those
who came after him, also proclaimed these
days. **25** You are the sons of the prophets and of the
covenant that God made with your fathers, saying to
Abraham, 'And in your offspring shall all the families
of the earth be blessed.' **26** God, having raised up his
servant, sent him to you first, to bless you by turning
every one of you from your wickedness." (Acts
3.17-26)

*How does the Revelation teach about the present blessing and
hope for those who have been raised with Christ?*

As I said it is a central truth given to us in the Revelation.
The glorious visions of the reign of our Lord and praises given
to him are about the reign of Christ since his glorious ascension. The Lord Jesus has been proclaimed king and rules at the
right hand of God. He is our great high priest of the order of
"Melchizedek" who is "king" and also "priest". In fact, his

name in the book of Genesis means "king of justice". As written in the letter to the Hebrews Melchizedek was a prefiguration of the King and High priest Jesus who rules today and will return in glory, the one who is "the faithful witness, the first-born from the dead and the ruler of kings on earth" (1.5). This Lord also made us a "kingdom and priests to his God and Father" (1.6). Our glorious Lord "is coming with the clouds and everyone will see him" (1.7).

I remember that the Lord is the one of whom the Psalms said, "You are a priest forever, after the order of Melchizedek." (Psalm 110.4; Hebrews 7.17). So, tell me more how the Revelation portrays the glory already given to the saints, to the Church of our Lord?

The Revelation provides many pictures of the glory already given to the saints. The living creatures around God's throne proclaim this truth when the lamb takes the scroll to open it:

"**8** And when he had taken the scroll, the four living creatures and the twenty-four elders fell down before the Lamb, each holding a harp, and golden bowls full of incense, which are the prayers of the saints. **9** And they sang a new song, saying,

'Worthy are you to take the scroll
and to open its seals,
for you were slain, and by your blood you ransomed people for God, and you have made them a kingdom and priests to our God,
and they shall reign on the earth.'" (Revelation 5.8-10)

The saints who come out of the great tribulation have "washed their robes and made them white in the blood of the lamb:

> **15** "Therefore they are before the throne of God,
>   and serve him day and night in his temple;
>   and he who sits on the throne will shelter them with
> his presence.
> **16** They shall hunger no more, neither thirst anymore;
>   the sun shall not strike them,
>   nor any scorching heat.
> **17** For the Lamb in the midst of the throne will be their
> shepherd,
>   and he will guide them to springs of living water,
> and God will wipe away every tear from their eyes
> (Revelation 7.16,17)

These words remind me of the teachings of our Lord to the Samaritan woman as he was speaking about the salvation and gift of God's Holy Spirit that would be poured on God's people:

> "**13** Jesus said to her, 'Everyone who drinks of this wa-
> ter will be thirsty again, **14** but whoever drinks of the
> water that I will give him will never be thirsty
> again. The water that I will give him will become in
> him a spring of water welling up to eternal
> life.' **15** The woman said to him, 'Sir, give me this wa-
> ter, so that I will not be thirsty or have to come here to
> draw water.'" (John 4.13,15)

Similar words were preached by our Lord in the temple on the last day of the feast:

> "**37** On the last day of the feast, the great day, Jesus
> stood up and cried out, 'If anyone thirsts, let him come

to me and drink. **38** Whoever believes in me, as the Scripture has said, 'Out of his heart will flow rivers of living water.'" (John 7.37,38). Our Lord Jesus said these words about the Spirit, "whom those who believed in him were to receive, for as yet the Spirit had not been given, because Jesus was not yet glorified." (John 7.39)

Is this not also found at the end of the Revelation about the "water of life", when the Lord calls all who are thirsty for righteousness and eternal life?

Yann, these are some of the last words of the Revelation when the Lord calls all to himself:

16 "I, Jesus, have sent my angel to testify to you about these things for the churches. I am the root and the descendant of David, the bright morning star." **17** The Spirit and the Bride say, 'Come.' And let the one who hears say, 'Come.' And let the one who is thirsty come; let the one who desires take the water of life without price." (Revelation 22.16,17)

3. TRIBULATIONS

"I, John, your brother and partner in the tribulation and the kingdom and the patient endurance that are in Jesus, was on the island called Patmos on account of the word of God and the testimony of Jesus." (Revelation 1.9)

*

John, how did you end up on this island?

Yann, since the reign of Nero opposition to the Lord Jesus and his teachings has greatly increased among the Roman rulers.

With the other apostles we were sharing in the last supper when the Lord warned us saying: "In the world you will have tribulation. But take heart; I have overcome the world" (John 16.33). He also said to us "Truly, truly I say to you, you will weep and lament, but the world will rejoice. You will be sorrowful, but your sorrow will turn into joy. When a woman is giving birth, she has sorrow because her hour has come, but when she has delivered the baby, she no longer remembers the anguish, for joy that a human being has been born into the world." (John 16.20,21).

Several years after the Lord's ascension I lived in Ephesus. The Lord had told me that I would live a long life. (John 21.20-25). I am now an older man and exiled on the isle of Patmos under the rule of emperor Vespasian. I was exiled on this island on account of the word of God and the testimony of Jesus. In the Revelation we see the rulers of Rome — the Babylon of today — as seven heads of the beast which carries the harlot, and which sits on seven mountains. (17.9)

This book of visions the Lord asked you to write is called by many "Revelation" ("Apocalypse). What is the meaning of this word?

The Greek word for Revelation, *apokalupsis*, is used at the very beginning of the book, "The revelation of Jesus Christ, which God gave him to show to his servants the things that must soon take place." (1.1) This word is used a number of times in the writings of the new covenant by Luke and the apostles Peter and Paul. (For example, Luke 2.32; 1 Peter 1.7; Romans 2.5). A "revelation" is a truth that was not known or that was hidden before but is now made visible and known. God in our Scriptures is the one who "reveals" what was not known before.

You mentioned Nero and Vespasian. Why mention these emperors and what can you tell us about them? What is your life like here in Patmos and has the Lord given you any revelation concerning your own future?

The brethren in Ephesus and the cities in Asia have known opposition to the faith from the very beginning. Our brother Luke, companion of Paul, records in his "Acts of Apostles" the difficult beginnings of the Church in Ephesus and how Paul spoke boldly in the Synagogue, "reasoning and persuading the things concerning the kingdom of God". (Acts 19:8). Luke records the fact that Paul taught in the school of Tyrannus for two years so that all the residents of Asia heard the word of the Lord both Jews and Gentiles. (Acts 19.9,10). This happened during the last two years of the rule of emperor Claudius. The adopted son of Claudius was Nero who succeeded him as emperor. It was under Nero that Paul was in Rome and was martyred there as well as Peter. Nero seized many of our brothers and sisters and had them killed by dogs by having hides of beasts attached to them. Others were nailed to crosses and set aflame. This lasted for about four years until Nero killed himself. Whatever the emperor decides in Rome is felt immediately in the Empire and has an influence on the actions of the proconsuls. In the Revelation given to me by the Lord he has shown me and the brethren that the terrible and persecuting beast in the prophecy of Daniel is the empire in the person of Nero and succeeding emperors. In Revelation the same beast has also ten horns and seven heads. (See Daniel 7.7,8 and Revelation 17.7-14). The seven heads represent rulers who were the first emperors of Rome. The seven heads are also the seven hills on which Rome was built. In the Revelation, the ten horns are also rulers who receive authority alongside the beast. Concerning my own future, I have already lived a long life and all my friends the apostles have died. As our brother and apostle Paul would have said "I have fought the good fight. I have finished the race. I have kept the faith. Henceforth there is laid up for me the crown of righteousness, which the Lord, the righteous judge, will award to me on that day; and not only to me but also to all who have loved his appearing". (2 Timothy 4.7,8).

*

My exile on this lost island is not a surprise for us. With Rome, exile usually means waiting for a death sentence. This happened to the apostle Paul under the rule of Nero. I miss the fellowship and communion of our brethren. But my future is safe in the Lord's hand who had taught us saying "if anyone enters by me, he will be saved and will go in and out and find pasture… My sheep hear my voice, and I know them, and they follow me. I give them eternal life and they will never perish, and no one will snatch them out of my hand." (John 10.9,27,28).

I pray the Lord in my soul constantly for my brethren, for the churches. I have been away from them for a few years and the Lord has just revealed to me that these churches dear to my heart have lost some battles against the evil one. The Lord has told me to address this letter with all of its visions to seven churches in Asia. The brethren in Ephesus have endured opposition and have not grown weary; they have continued to do a lot of good works, but the Lord has told me that they have abandoned the love they had at first. (2.3,4).

John, but if they have endured opposition and have worked hard for the Lord Jesus what does it mean that they have abandoned the love they had at first?

Remember, Yann the words of our dear apostle Paul: "If I speak in the tongues of men and of angels, but have not love, I am a noisy gong or a clanging cymbal. And if I have prophetic powers, and understand all mysteries and all knowledge, and if I have all faith, so as to remove mountains, but have not love, I am nothing. If I give away all I have, and if I deliver up my body to be burned, but have not love, I gain nothing." (1 Corinthians 13.1-3). Remember also the teachings of the apostle Paul concerning the gift of the Holy Spirit and how the wonderful fruit of that gift is first described by the word "love", followed by joy and peace (Galatians 5.22-25).

Yes, I remember those words written to the Christians in Corinth and also to the brethren in the region of Galatia. It is still difficult for me to understand how one can endure opposition for the Lord and even work hard for the spread of the Gospel while having in fact abandoned the love commanded by the Lord.

One day my brother James and I were coming through a village of the Samaritans as we were headed to Jerusalem. But these Samaritans refused to receive Jesus. Angry at them, we asked the Lord "Do you want us to tell fire to come down from heaven and consume them?" But the Lord rebuked us for our reaction, and we went to another village (Luke 9.54,55). We loved the Lord and did not want him to be mistreated. Not showing hospitality to our Lord was in our eyes so shameful and deserved punishment by death. Jesus rebuked us and we remembered how he taught us to love our enemies and bless them, to even pray for them. (Matthew 5.43-48). When the Lord revealed to me how the brethren in Ephesus faced opposition but also had abandoned their first love, I understood why the Lord was also rebuking them. We cannot claim to love the Lord Jesus if we hate or mistreat anyone or wish them death.

I understand. What the Lord is saying to the Church in Ephesus is so true even today. We cannot pretend to love the Lord and want to serve him, while neglecting the love of our neighbor and even of our enemies. But we need to strive to keep those two great commandments together as Jesus taught us himself.

As we walked with Jesus and witnessed his love for God and for people, we learned from him what some of our rabbis already believed: before and above everything else we must love

God and love our neighbor as ourselves. This was taught to us in the Torah first in the book of Deuteronomy and also in the book of Leviticus. (Deuteronomy 6.4-9 and Leviticus 19.17,18. Matthew 22.36-40).

During the last supper our Lord taught us to abide in his love, saying "If you keep my commandments, you will abide in my love, just as I have kept my Father's commandments and abide in his love." (John 15.10). He also told us that "whoever has my commandments and keeps them, he is who loves me" and added "Whoever does not love me does not keep my words." (John 15.21, 24). If someone hates his brother or his neighbor that he sees how can he pretend to love God or Jesus our Lord that he does not see? And remember that Jesus taught us from the very beginning that his disciples are called to be light to the world and salt of the earth.

This is why in the first vision I received from him he is standing in the midst of seven golden lampstands. These lampstands are a reminder of the lampstand placed by Moses in the Tabernacle. This lampstand described in the book of Exodus was made of solid gold. (Exodus 25.31-39; 37. 17-24). It had a central column and six branches extending on each side. The lampstand was an oil lamp needed to bring light in the Holy place — a place where there should never be any darkness because God is light and there is no darkness in him. And as there is no darkness in God, we are also called to have no darkness in our lives; disciples and churches must walk in the light as he is in the light. This means they should avoid all sin, and if they sin, they should repent and confess this to God who will forgive them (1 John 1.7-10).

John, do you have people who do not think they sin or can sin? Today we have people, even among believers, who believe this and do not consider sin as an important issue with God.

Even now there are false teachers who teach wrongly that we cannot sin; others teach that if we sin that is not a big issue with God since he is gracious to us in Jesus Christ. These false teachings on sin are mentioned in many places in the epistles of Paul and Peter and others as well as in my own epistles as in the first where I write the following: **"5** This is the message we have heard from him and declare to you: God is light; in him there is no darkness at all. **6** If we claim to have fellowship with him and yet walk in the darkness, we lie and do not live out the truth. **7** But if we walk in the light, as he is in the light, we have fellowship with one another, and the blood of Jesus, his Son, purifies us from all sin. **8** If we claim to be without sin, we deceive ourselves and the truth is not in us. **9** If we confess our sins, he is faithful and just and will forgive us our sins and purify us from all unrighteousness. **10** If we claim we have not sinned, we make him out to be a liar and his word is not in us." (1 John 1.5-10).

The Lord has found these false teachings also spreading in some of the seven churches of Asia and has shown this to me in his Revelation. (Revelation chapters 2 and 3). The Lord calls these churches and individuals to repent from their wrong teachings and from their sins.

John, there was one lampstand in the tabernacle but in this vision, we have seven lampstands. Why the difference?

These were his words written for us by my brother in the faith and apostle Matthew: "You are the light of the world. A city set on a hill cannot be hidden. Nor do people light a lamp and put it under a basket, but on a stand, and it gives light to all in the house. In the same way, let your light shine before others, so that they may see your good works and give glory to your Father who is in heaven." (Matthew 5.14,15). In the Revelation the Lord repeats what our fathers have been teaching for generations and also what he himself taught us on the mount. In our book of Proverbs, we are reminded that "the path of the righteous is like the light of dawn, which shines brighter and brighter until full day. The way of the wicked is like deep darkness; they do not know over what they stumble." (Proverbs 4.18). So, our Lord himself taught us to be light to the world and not to hide that light. Yes, we had a lampstand in the tabernacle and one in the temple, but that meant that as a people we needed to be light to the world. It also meant that light among our people could only come from God himself and from the Messiah he would send us. In the Revelation there are seven lampstands because this book was first addressed to seven churches in Asia mentioned in the beginning of the book. Each church is to be a light to the world around. Light is the message we heard from our Lord and are now proclaiming to the world. This message says that God is light and there is no darkness in him. We need to walk in the light and not just talk or preach about it. Yes, we all sin but when we do sin, we need to come to the Lord and talk to him, seeking his forgiveness. Because he is faithful and righteous, he will not only forgive our sins but even cleanse us from all unrighteousness. (1 John 1.5-10). Our fellowship with the Lord and with each other depends on this.

*

John, I remember how often you talk about light in your Gospel and in your letters. But I have also read about the meaning of light in the Psalms and other Scriptures. Could you share more about light to those of us who live now two thousand years later?

Yann, as you know at the time of the Exodus from Egypt under Moses, God who is the eternal and glorious light of our universe instructed us to place a lampstand which we call *menorah*, in the holy place of the tabernacle, the tent where our people and priests met with God. There was only one menorah in the tabernacle and later in the temple. But you notice that in the vision there are seven menorahs, one in each town where Jesus' followers meet together to break bread, worship the Lord and learn from his word. The menorah in Ephesus brings light to the people of that city as do the other menorahs in the other cities mentioned by the Lord. Our brethren in Ephesus had in the past received a letter from the apostle Paul who taught them also about the importance of shining the light of God and truth through our lives when he instructed them saying,

"Therefore be imitators of God, as beloved children. **2** And walk in love as Christ loved us and gave himself up for us, a fragrant offering and sacrifice to God." (Ephesians 5.1,2). "**8** for at one time you were darkness, but now you are light in the Lord. Walk as children of light **9** (for the fruit of light is found in all that is good and right and true), **10** and try to discern what is pleasing to the Lord." (Ephesians 5.8-10).

But now I am in grief, my heart is burdened by the words concerning my brothers and sisters in Ephesus when the Jesus our Lord said to them, "But I have this against you, that you have abandoned the love you had at first. Remember therefore from where you have fallen; repent and do the works you did at first. If not, I will come to you and remove your lampstand from its place, unless you repent." (2.4,5)

I noticed in the vision that the lampstands are these churches but Jesus himself is not a lampstand. He stands in the middle of the lampstands. (1.12,13).

Yes, and not only that but he is dressed like a priest "with a long robe and with a golden sash on his chest". (1.13). Jesus is not a lampstand among others because he is himself the light of all of these churches and the light of the world as he taught himself. (John 8.12). In the vision Jesus our Lord stands as the priests stood in the holy place in order to intercede on behalf of the people who could not enter close to the presence of God. But the vision shows us that Jesus our priest stands with the lampstands around him, that there is no barrier, no veil, between the priest and the people who come to God through him. This is what our brother who wrote Hebrews is teaching us: "Since we have confidence to enter the holy places by the blood of Jesus by the new and living way that he opened for us through the curtain, that is through his flesh, and since we have a great priest over the house of God, let us draw near with a true heart in full assurance of faith, with our hearts sprinkled from an evil conscience and our bodies washed with pure water." (Hebrews 10.19-22).

John, we live over two thousand years after the vision was given to you. Is the Lord speaking to us in this revelation, this unveiling, you received from the Lord?

Jesus made it clear from the start of this revelation that he was showing me "things that must soon take place" and he stated also "Blessed is the one who reads aloud the words of this prophecy and blessed are those who hear and who keep what is written in it, for the time is near" (1.1). The Lord repeated this at the end of the revelation, saying to me "Do not seal up the words of the prophecy of this book, for the time is near" (22.10).

Does this mean that this revelation is only for those who lived when the Lord gave it? How do we know the Lord is speaking also to us in these visions?

The Revelation is for all who will read it and apply it in their lives. We understand this especially when we are attentive to the last words of this revelation. The warnings and visions of this revelation are to be read and listened to until the Lord returns and rewards each one for what he has done: "Behold, I am coming soon, bringing my recompense with me to repay each one for what he has done". (22.12). The one who speaks like this is the Lord who is also the "Alpha and the Omega, the first and the last, the beginning and the end" (22.13).

When he says the "last" and the "end" he is including all peoples of all times, all Christians of all times until he returns in glory. The warnings and visions given to me and the seven churches are to be taken to heart and are to be obeyed by all peoples until the Lord returns in his glory. Remember also the words of the Lord when I received the little scroll from the mighty angel: "You must again prophesy about many peoples and nations and languages and kings."

John, is this Revelation about kings or rulers that have lived and died over the centuries or present kings and rulers? How should we understand this?

The Revelation does not give names and does not describes these rulers throughout the entire world and throughout time until the Lord returns. The beast that comes out of the sea and makes war against God's people and humanity is not just one specific individual whether in the past or future. It is simply the "number of man" which is 666. (Revelation 13.18). This number 666 points to human beings exercising worldly powers, to rulers such as the emperors always at risk of forgetting their humanity; forgetting that they are only human beings and not to be worshipped or relied on as God would. This teaching of the Revelation is not so different from the failures and sins of so many of the ancient kings of Israel: "The sons of Israel walked in all the sins of Jeroboam which he did; they did not depart from them until the Lord removed Israel from His sight, as He spoke through all His servants the prophets. So, Israel was carried away into exile from their own land to Assyria until this day," (2 Kings 17.21-23).

Man was created on the 6th day, the day that precedes the 7th which is the day the entire creation was completed as also reflected in the "sabbath" later given to our people as a commandment. Man cannot reach divine completeness and perfection and he must recognize this fact. It is difficult for those who have received power and authority to remain humble and at the service of others. This is what our Lord continually taught us during his ministry and teaches us in His word. (Matthew 20.25; Philippians 2.1-5).

In the Revelation remember that the Lord announced to John that "the time is near". The Revelation mentions the rulers or kings of Rome represented by the heads and horns of the beast that carries the harlot, Babylon drunk with the blood of the saints. (13.1-9; 17.1-14). The seven heads of the beast are also seven mountains and seven kings who are responsible for murdering the saints. They make war on the lamb. The Lord wants us to understand that "war on the lamb" will continue until the Lord returns in glory.

But what does Babylon have to do with these rulers at war with the Christ and who persecute the saints?

Remember how the book of Genesis tells the story of Nimrod who founded Babel, a city and construction defiant of God and his authority and power. (Genesis 11.4-9). The founders of Babel wanted to make a name for themselves. They wanted to exercise more and more power over more and more people. God said about these rulers, "This is only the beginning of what they will do. And nothing that they propose to do will now be impossible for them." (Genesis 11.6). Remember how our prophet Daniel was himself in captivity under Babylon and how this great power crushed our people. The rulers of Babylon gave their city this name which means "gate of the gods" because they believed that Babylon was the central place where the gods consorted with humans to order the affairs of the earth.

The story about Babel and the behavior of Babylon has remained examples of arrogance and pride which God has always opposed. Through the prophet Daniel God left us a message about how he views the arrogance of men in their opposition to his will. In the dream of Nebuchadnezzar about the great statue, the king of Babylon saw four great empires covering the earth until the stone came and crushed all of these empires, even the last empire of iron mixed with clay. The prophecy told us that in the days of the kings belonging to this last empire God would set up his kingdom which would never be destroyed, and which is the kingdom of the Messiah who in prophecy is the stone that God has established for his people. (Isaiah 28.16).

In the dream the stone itself became a kingdom that spread all over the earth. (Daniel chapter 2). This last empire of Daniel is also the fourth beast of Daniel's prophecy, a beast with iron teeth and also ten horns as in the Revelation. This beast is the empire of Rome. As in the Revelation one of the horns has a mouth that speaks great things and makes war against the saints. This is the emperor who claims to be a god and wants to be worshipped (Daniel 7.7,8,21).

In this case John what does the Lord mean when he says in the Revelation: "You must again prophesy about many peoples and nations and languages and kings."? (Revelation 10.11)

The arrogance on the part of the founders of Babel and the rulers of Babylon is not different from the behavior of the horns and heads of Rome which is the fourth empire in the prophecies of Daniel. This behavior is no different from the heads of the beast in the Revelation. And this behavior is no different from what happens with rulers of the world until the return of our Lord.

John, how can this Revelation concern "prophecy" that is about what is to happen during your lifetime and about future nations and rulers if those nations and rulers are not mentioned specifically?

As we continue this dialogue you will understand why this is the case. You will see that this is really the case for most of our Scriptures and even for the inspired writings of Jesus' prophets and apostles. Thus, this is a question we will continually come back to and you will see how the Lord reveals truth to Christians and churches of the future and also to nations and rulers of the future; how the Lord reveals to them what they need to know and what they need to do.

Our prophets were inspired to teach and warn our people. We learn of kings and rulers outside of Israel which are mentioned in the first testament and we learn of kings in the Revelation. But who they are, their names and the details of their existence are mostly absent from the Scriptures. What is really important is to understand how God views their behavior and their pride. But when our Scriptures prophesy about the Messiah, the Anointed of God, we find a wealth of information. We are taught that this savior and ruler would be a man of the seed of woman; we are taught that he would come from the tribe of

Judah and would descend from David. We are also told that he would be born in Bethlehem and would perform great miracles. Our prophets spoke of his death, his resurrection and his rule at the right hand of God. Our Psalms talked about his rule and judgments over the nations. (Psalms 2). And the Revelation confirms his rule and authority over the nations until he returns, and his kingdom is made manifest to all and he brings about the new heaven and new earth.

John, you are in exile and all the other apostles have gone to be with the Lord. I remember reading in Luke's book of Acts that Judas was replaced because he betrayed the Lord. What will happen to the church when you have passed away? How will the churches continue in the faith without the apostles and their teaching?

The answer to this question is that the Lord Jesus will continue to teach his disciples and churches through the word he has given to us. In this Revelation as in all of Scripture the Lord is speaking to his people. I was told to write what I saw in a book and send it to the seven churches. (1.11). The angel who came to me on this island was bearing witness to the word of God and to the testimony of Jesus Christ. (1.2). God pronounces a blessing on "those who hear and who keep what is written in it, for the time is near" (1.3).

This is similar to what I wrote at the end of my Gospel, that these things were written "that you may believe that Jesus is the Christ, the Son of God, and that by believing you may have life in his name". (John 20.30,31). You live in a far distant future, but you know what God has revealed to his prophets and apostles; you have the Scripture which are "God-breathed and profitable for teaching, for reproof, for correction and for training in righteousness, that the man of God may be complete, equipped for every good work" as our brother Paul wrote to

Timothy. (2 Timothy 3.16). The God of our father Abraham, the God of Moses and the prophets has chosen his people to consign and preserve as well as teach the Scriptures he has inspired and revealed. This is what Jesus expects of his people and he provides gifts of teaching and leading to the church so that his word can be taught, so that the church can grow in love and unity. This is also what the apostle Paul wrote to our Ephesian brethren in his letter to them. (Ephesians 4.9-16).

But having these Scriptures and understanding their meaning is not enough. The real challenge for God's people is not simply in outside circumstances, empires that rise and fall. The challenge for God's people is the one the Church in Ephesus is warned about by Jesus at the very beginning of the Revelation:

> "**2** I know your works, your toil and your patient endurance, and how you cannot bear with those who are evil but have tested those who call themselves apostles and are not and found them to be false. **3** I know you are enduring patiently and bearing up for my name's sake, and you have not grown weary. **4** But I have this against you, that you have abandoned the love you had at first. **5** Remember therefore from where you have fallen; repent and do the works you did at first. If not, I will come to you and remove your lampstand from its place, unless you repent." (Revelation 2.2-5).

*

The practice of the greatest and new commandment "love one another" is a greater challenge than all exterior forces that come against the Church. The Holy Spirit was given to us in order to produce its fruit. For the Church in Ephesus and the Church of the present and future until the return of Christ the greatest challenge is the greatest commandment left by our

Lord which He has himself given me to write about in my three letters as what I wrote in the first of these letters:

> "**7** Beloved, I am writing you no new commandment, but an old commandment that you had from the beginning. The old commandment is the word that you have heard. **8** At the same time, it is a new commandment that I am writing to you, which is true in him and in you, because the darkness is passing away and the true light is already shining. **9** Whoever says he is in the light and hates his brother is still in darkness. **10** Whoever loves his brother abides in the light, and in him there is no cause for stumbling. **11** But whoever hates his brother is in the darkness and walks in the darkness, and does not know where he is going, because the darkness has blinded his eyes." (1 John 2.7-11).

But John in the Revelation the church in Ephesus is showing signs of unfaithfulness. How can an unfaithful church or unfaithful disciples carry out the task of preserving and teaching the word of God? How will this happen especially if the Lord says to the church "I will remove your lampstand from its place unless you repent"?

What you mention here is no different from the disobedience and sin we find among our people Israel in the Old Testament. This disobedience was such that the northern tribes were taken to Assyria and later the tribe of Judah was taken into exile to Babylon. Does this mean that the word God had given to his prophets was forever lost and that absolutely no one was going to teach that word? The history of our people shows us that this is not what happened, even when the law appeared to be completely forgotten and ignored. Remember that after 57 years of the rule of evil kings Manasseh and Amon the law which had been ignored was found in the temple by Hilkiah the high priest who gave it to Shaphan, the secretary. He then read the law to king Josiah who tore his robes. (2 Kings 22). Josiah himself had never read the book of the law but it was preserved.

To my brethren the Israelites has been given the law, as Paul wrote to the Christians in Rome. (Romans 9.4). And despite all the unfaithfulness of kings and the people God has preserved his word and has sent prophets to remind the people of God's word. We need to remember the promise of Jesus who told us that "heaven and earth will pass away, but my words will not pass away". (Matthew 24.35).

Despite unfaithful churches and unfaithful believers, the Lord in his power and providence does not and will not allow his word to be completely extinct and ignored. As it was the case with our people Israel the truth of God's word will continue to be known and taught even if through a small faithful remnant or a few prophets here and there. Maybe we are sometimes like Elijah who thought he was the only prophet left who was faithful to God but was told: "Yet I will leave seven thousand in Israel, all the knees that have not bowed to Baal." (1 Kings 19.18) I will die as the other apostles of our Lord have died but the truth of God's word and our testimony and teachings as apostles will last. The faith we preach has been delivered to the saints "once for all" as brother Jude writes in his epistle. (Jude v.3).

The apostle Paul wrote to Timothy that he was convinced the Lord is able to guard until that day what had been entrusted to him. So, Timothy was taught to "follow the pattern of sound words" that he had heard from the apostle. (2 Timothy 1.12,13). Remember that Timothy was the evangelist in Ephesus for many years. Timothy has passed away and now the

Church in Ephesus is in danger of straying away from the truth and even in danger of losing its light because it has forgotten its "first love". But the good works of Paul the apostle and Timothy are preserved by God. This is also confirmed in the Revelation: "Here is a call for the endurance of the saints, those who keep the commandments of God and their faith in Jesus. And I heard a voice from heaven saying, 'Write this: Blessed are the dead who die in the Lord from now on.' 'Blessed indeed,' says the Spirit, 'that they may rest from their labors, for their deeds follow them!'" (Revelation 14.12,13)

*

John, I am struck by the fact that these seven cities mentioned in the Revelation and located in our modern Turkey are for the most part ruins today while the name of Jesus is proclaimed all over the world almost two thousand years later.

Cities and buildings made by human hands cannot last forever. It was even prophecied by the Lord Jesus that the temple would be destroyed. (Matthew 24). In this Revelation given by the Lord we see none of the fame, glory and wealth of these seven cities. The Lord only addresses those who live in these cities and who claim to follow him and live for him. Ephesus is today one of the largest cities of the entire Roman empire. The amphitheater can hold up to 25,000 people. It is a wealthy city and people come from all over the world to worship in the temple of Artemis.

Yes John, and even today we can see the ruins of this large amphitheater.

Smyrna is an important commercial city with a famous marketplace. It is also a very ancient town, older than any other mentioned by the Lord in the Revelation. But as in the case of Ephesus the Lord speaks to those who are disciples there and many of whom are very poor and under great tribulation for their faith in the Lord Jesus.

Today the town's name is Izmir and it is a very large city. One can still see the ruins of the marketplace there.

Pergamum is also an important city for the Romans. It is from Pergamum that the proconsul of Rome rules over Asia. The steep theater built on the side of a hill can hold up to 10,000 spectators. The town also has one of the largest libraries in the world. The town has a famous temple called the Augustan Temple dedicated to the emperor. There is also a temple dedicated to the worship of Zeus. From a great distance, travelers can see the smoke of sacrifices offered constantly to the god from the top of the hill. The worship of Asklepios is also important to the city. The sick come from everywhere with the hope of being healed by this pagan god. This is why the Revelation describes Pergamum as "where Satan dwells". In his first letter to the Church in Corinth the apostle Paul reminds the followers of Jesus that those who participate in offerings or sacrifices to pagan gods in fact are "participants with demons". (1 Corinthians 10.18-21)

I read that the Lord speaking to Pergamum warned those Christians that they should not eat food sacrificed to idols and practice sexual immorality.

These things are practiced by the majority of those who live in Pergamum and these other towns of Asia just like in Corinth and the entire world under the Roman rule. The Romans are not troubled by these practices or these sins and which are even part of the worship of the Greek and Roman gods. But they have caused great pains to our people Israel in the past and now to the followers of the Christ.

What about Thyatira? The name of the city today is Akhisar and it has a population of 100,000. There are almost no ruins of ancient Thyatira today in Akhisar.

The city is known for its bronze workers. In the vision Jesus shows himself with "feet like burnished bronze". Lydia who was converted by the preaching of the apostle Paul in Philippi came from Thytira. She was a merchant of purple goods, an important trade in Thyatira. Our brethren there need "patient endurance" mentioned by our Lord because of the worship of idols and also the many guilds attached to the festivities and worship of these gods and required of these merchants. Our Lord speaks in his letter to this church of those who think they have a deeper knowledge and are not troubled by participating in idolatrous practices and worship. But the Lord says he is the one who has a "deeper knowledge" and who searches the mind and the heart; his disciples must "hold fast" to what they have received from the Lord.

Today Sardis is called Sart. The town of 5,000 residents is full of excavations. I learned that legendary king Croesus who amassed so much gold was from Sardis.

Sardis is one of the wealthiest cities of Asia and even the Roman world. Just like Laodicea the wealth of the city has produced a growing weakness of their faith among the Christians and the Lord is warning them with these words: "Wake up and strengthen what remains and is about to die. I have not found your works complete in the sight of my God. Remember, then, what you received and heard. Keep it, and repent." (3.2,3). As with Sardis the town of Laodicea mentioned by the Lord is also a wealthy city.

Colossae and Laodicea are towns close to Sardis. The apostle Paul wrote a letter to Colossae which he instructed should also be read in Laodicea. (Colossians 4.16). At the time of this letter

Paul was encouraged by the strong faith in Christ of those Christians. (Colossians 2.5). As happens often when people gain more wealth and independence their commitment to Christ weakens. They need to become once again listeners to the call of the Lord who "stands and knocks at the door" of the human heart, saying, "If anyone hears my voice and opens the door, I will come in to him and eat with him and he with me. The one who conquers, I will grant him to sit with me on my throne, as I also conquered and sat down with my Father on his throne. He who has an ear, let him hear what the Spirit says to the churches." (3.20-22).

I noticed that the Lord has only praises for his followers in Philadelphia, the city of "brotherly love".

This church is a great example of faithfulness to the Lord for the other cities in Asia and even Christians all over the Roman world. The city is also known by the name Flavia in honor of emperor Vespasian. The city is a center of worship of the god Dionysios (Bacchus for the Romans), the god of wine. The area is known for its production of grapes and many vineyards. The Christians in Philadelphia are still faithful, they have kept the word of the Lord and have not denied his name. The Lord who speaks to this Church is "the holy one, the true one, who has the key of David, who opens and no one will shut, who shuts and no one opens". (3.7). The holy one describes the Messiah as mentioned in my own Gospel in the words of Peter, "We have believed and have come to know that you are the holy one of God". (John 6.68). He is also the true one as he taught us himself: he is the "true" light, "true bread" and also "true vine".

*

Yet no human effort, no princely largess nor offerings to the gods could make that infamous rumor disappear that Nero had somehow ordered the fire. Therefore, in order to abolish that rumor, Nero falsely accused and executed with the most exquisite punishments those people called Christians, who were infamous for their abominations. The originator of the name, Christ, was executed as a criminal by the procurator Pontius Pilate during the reign of Tiberius; and though repressed, this destructive superstition erupted again, not only through Judea, which was the origin of this evil, but also through the city of Rome, to which all that is horrible and shameful floods together and is celebrated. Therefore, first those were seized who admitted their faith, and then, using the information they provided, a vast multitude were convicted, not so much for the crime of burning the city, but for hatred of the human race. And perishing they were additionally made into sports: they were killed by dogs by having the hides of beasts attached to them, or they were nailed to crosses or set aflame, and, when the daylight passed away, they were used as nighttime lamps.[1]

---

[1]*TACITUS (55-117 AD), Translated by Richard Hooker, 07/30/21https://brians.wsu.edu/2016/11/14/tacitus-neros-persecution-of-the-christians/*

4. FEAR NOT

"Fear not, I am the first and the last, and the living one.
I died, and behold I am alive forevermore,
and I have the keys of Death and Hades." (Revelation
1.17,18)

*

*John, I remember that the words of the Lord saying "Fear not"
are also found throughout the Scriptures. Why are these words
always so important throughout God's dealings with his people
and with nations?*

Yes, this is true. These words are constantly spoken by God
to the faithful and to his prophets. When I received the first vision, I saw our Lord as the Son of man and fell at his feet like
dead: "His eyes were like a flame of fire, his feet were like
burnished bronze, refined in a furnace, and his voice was like
the roar of many waters." (1.14,15).

Is not this what happened to the prophet Daniel?

Daniel describes in his book the "man clothed in linen": "His body was like beryl, his face like the appearance of lightning, his eyes like flaming torches, his arms and legs like the gleam of burnished bronze, and the sound of his words like the sound of a multitude." (Daniel 10.6). When Daniel saw Him, he fell at his feet as dead. (Daniel 1.17). The "son of man" I saw in the Revelation spoke to me words of comfort as were spoken to Daniel: "Fear not, I am the first and the last, and the living one. I died, and behold I am alive forevermore, and I have the keys of Death and Hades." (1.17). These words of comfort reminded me of the words spoken in the vision of Daniel: "O Daniel, man greatly loved, understand the words that I speak to you, and stand upright, for now I have been sent to you. Fear not, Daniel, for from the first day that you set your heart to understand and humbled yourself before your God, your words have been heard, and I have come because of your words." (Daniel 10.11,12). The visions given to me in the Revelation were often terrifying, but the Lord continually comforted me and encouraged me not be fearful just as Daniel was comforted in the midst of terrifying visions: "O man greatly loved fear not, peace be with you; be strong and of good courage." And as he spoke to me, I was strengthened and said, "Let my lord speak, for you have strengthened me." (Daniel 10.19).

In the Revelation this was the first time that my resurrected Lord showed himself and spoke in this manner. It was terrifying even for me. But as soon as he spoke, I was comforted by his words. He told me that these fearful visions were not given to me to produce fear in my heart but to write them down — "those that are and those that are to take place after this". (1.19 and 11). The power and glory of the one I saw in the Revelation made my entire body tremble to the point I could not stand up and immediately fell down at his feet. But his words immediately comforted me and gave me the strength to endure more of these terrifying visions.

So, John in this Revelation do you mean that there are terrifying visions and words but also comforting visions and words?

Yes, Yann. These are like two sides of the same coin. Remember also what is written in the Revelation about the little scroll in the hands of the mighty angel and how I was told to eat the scroll: "Then the voice that I had heard from heaven spoke to me again, saying, 'Go, take the scroll that is open in the hand of the angel who is standing on the sea and on the land.' So, I went to the angel and told him to give me the little scroll. And he said to me, 'Take and eat it; it will make your stomach bitter, but in your mouth, it will be sweet as honey.' And I took the little scroll from the hand of the angel and ate it. It was sweet as honey in my mouth, but when I had eaten it my stomach was made bitter. And I was told, 'You must again prophesy about many peoples and nations and languages and kings.'" When I heard these words of the angel "Take and eat" I remembered what our Scriptures have taught us about the prophet Ezekiel. God spoke to the prophet who was already in the captivity of Babylonia and gave him "bitter" but also "sweet" revelations about the future of His people Israel. (Ezekiel chapter 3). "Son of man, all my words that I shall speak to you receive in your heart and hear with your ears. 11 And go to the exiles, to your people, and speak to them and say to them, 'Thus says the Lord God,' whether they hear or refuse to hear."

When you were told by the angel to "eat" the little scroll this meant that you were to consider this word of God like food. Is this similar what the words of the law quoted by Jesus in his temptation, that "man shall not live by bread alone"?

The manna given by God to Israel in the desert was not something they cultivated and made. It came directly from God and it was able to nourish them. This manna was a lesson to consider the food of God's word which is as necessary to live as the bread made by human hands: "And he humbled you and let you hunger and fed you with manna, which you did not know, nor did your fathers know, that he might make you know that man does not live by bread alone, but man lives by every word that comes from the mouth of the Lord." (Deuteronomy 8.3).

Would it be correct to say that in a sense the words revealed by God always contain this element of sweetness and bitterness?

The entire revelation of God, all of the Scriptures you yourself are reading, can build you up and encourage you but also can correct you and even judge you. The apostle Paul taught Timothy that the Scriptures are breathed by God and "profitable for teaching, for reproof, for correction, and for training in righteousness, **17** that the man of God may be complete, equipped for every good work." (2 Timothy 3.16,17). This is the case for all of our Scriptures and true for the Revelation given to me on Patmos as it was true for Ezekiel.

The correction and judgments of God have a bitter taste, but they are needed for the building up of our souls and hearts just as much as the comforting words given to us by God. Remember that in the law given to our people through Moses there were blessings as well as curses and that both needed to be read yearly by Israel so that they would not forget the law of God. In the book *devarim* [Deuteronomy] given through Moses, our people were taught to split up and stand on Mt. Gerizim and Mt. Ebal. They were to recite blessings from Gerizim and curses from Ebal. They should not forget these two sides of God's revelation.

So, in the Revelation there are also two sides to the visions and words you heard?

These two sides — blessings and curses — are to be remembered until the Lord returns for judgment. This is what is meant for example by some of the last words we find in the Revelation: "And he said to me, 'Do not seal up the words of the prophecy of this book, for the time is near. Let the evildoer still do evil, and the filthy still be filthy, and the righteous still do right, and the holy still be holy. Behold, I am coming soon, bringing my recompense with me, to repay each one for what he has done. I am the Alpha and the Omega, the first and the last, the beginning and the end. Blessed are those who wash their robes so that they may have the right to the tree of life and that they may enter the city by the gates. Outside are the dogs and sorcerers and the sexually immoral and murderers and idolaters, and everyone who loves and practices falsehood.'" (22.1-15)

This means that this Revelation is also about behavior and the condition of our hearts.

That is the case from the beginning; this is the message of the letters sent to each of the seven churches. These letters contain blessings and words of comfort as well as warnings. As all other Scriptures given to our people and to the Lord's apostles this is a Revelation to help God's people live holy lives before God, to repent if needed, to give up any sin that lingers in their hearts. God speaks to us in His word and we must put his word into practice. We must not be like those mentioned by James who hear the word but do not put it into practice: "like a man who looks intently at his natural face in a mirror. For he looks at himself and goes away and at once forgets what he was like." (James 1.23,24).

*

    1 The Lord is my light and my salvation;
        whom shall I fear?
    The Lord is the stronghold of my life;
        of whom shall I be afraid?
    2 When evildoers assail me
        to eat up my flesh,
    my adversaries and foes,
        it is they who stumble and fall.
    3 Though an army encamp against me,
        my heart shall not fear;
    though war arise against me,
        yet] I will be confident.
    4 One thing have I asked of the Lord,
        that will I seek after:
    that I may dwell in the house of the Lord
        all the days of my life,
    to gaze upon the beauty of the Lord
        and to inquire in his temple. (Psalms 27.1-4)

When the government of Nero was now firmly established, he began to plunge into unholy pursuits, and armed himself even against the religion of the God of the universe. To describe the greatness of his depravity does not lie within the plan of the present work. As there are many indeed that have recorded his history in most accurate narratives, every one may at his pleasure learn from them the coarseness of the man's extraordinary madness, under the influence of which, after he had accomplished the destruction of so many myriads without any reason, he ran into such blood-guiltiness that he did not spare even his nearest relatives and dearest friends, but destroyed his mother and his brothers and his wife, with very many others of his own family as he would private and public enemies, with various kinds of deaths. (Eusebius, Ecclesiastical History Book II. 25).

Domitian, having shown great cruelty toward many, and having unjustly put to death no small number of well-born and notable men at Rome, and having without cause exiled and confiscated the property of a great many other illustrious men, finally became a successor of Nero in his hatred and enmity toward God. He was in fact the second that stirred up a persecution against us.[1]

---

[1] Eusebius, *Ecclesiastical History* Book III.17

5. THE SON OF MAN

"Then I turned to see the voice that was speaking to me, and on turning I saw seven golden lampstands and in the midst of the lampstands one like a son of man, clothed with a long robe and with a golden sash around his chest." (Revelation 1.12,13)

*

Can you tell me more about how, in the Revelation, Jesus is the Son of man.

In the Revelation Jesus is called from the beginning "Son of man" in the first vision I received from him and later in the book in the great vision of the harvest of the earth: "Then I looked and behold a white cloud and seated on the cloud one like a son of man, with a golden crown on his head, and a sharp sickle in his hand." (14.14-20).

When the Lord preached and taught, he talked about himself more often than any other as being "the Son of man". When our Lord spoke this way, he did not mean that he was a man or

53

the son of a man. He was speaking of himself as the Messiah, the anointed one as Daniel had seen him in a vision. Exiled in Babylonia the prophet saw "a son of man" coming in power and glory for judgment upon the "four great beasts" that came out of the sea like a lion, a bear, a leopard and the last beast terrifying and dreadful with iron teeth and with ten horns. (Daniel chapter 7). Later in his life, under the rule of Cyrus of Persia, Daniel was mourning and fasting for three weeks after he had seen the vision of the seventy weeks. He saw in a vision a man "clothed in linen" and whose face was like the appearance of lightening and eyes like flaming torches. (Daniel chapter 10).

So, when Jesus was talking about himself as the son of man this had to do with Daniel's visions?

Jesus made this clear when he stood before the Great Sanhedrin after his arrestation. When the high priest asked him "Are you the Christ, the Son of the Blessed" our Lord answered saying "I am, and you will see the Son of Man seated at the right hand of Power and coming with the clouds of heaven." By saying these words Jesus was pointing to the vision of Messiah given to Daniel. In Matthew, Mark and Luke Jesus talks about himself as the "Son of man" many times. Stephen the martyr also saw Jesus as the Son of man when he said: "I see the heavens opened and the Son of man standing at the right hand of God". (Acts 7.56). Remember also that the Lord announced his coming in glory at the end of times as "the Son of man coming in clouds with great power and glory. And then he will send out the angels and gather his elect from the four winds, from the ends of the earth to the ends of heaven." (Mark 13.26,27).

What else can you tell me about the title Son of man in Jesus' ministry and in the Revelation?

When Jesus walked among us, he taught us that the Son of Man can forgive sins; that he is Lord of the Sabbath and that he came to save us and execute judgment; that he would rise from the dead. The letter to the Hebrews teaches our brethren the dignity and glory of the Son of Man, the Messiah who was once "made a little lower than the angels" but was crowned with glory and honor as our Psalms testified: "What is man, that you are mindful of him, or the son of man, that you care for him? You made him for a little while lower than the angels; you have crowned him with glory and honor, putting everything in subjection under his feet." (Psalms 8; Hebrews 1.6-8).

In the Revelation Jesus is clothed with a long robe and a golden sash around his chest. What is the meaning of this?

The Son of Man I saw in the Revelation resembles closely what Daniel tells us about his vision. In the vision given to Daniel the Son of Man is clothed in linen with a belt of fine gold from Uphaz around his waist. In the Revelation he has a long robe and a golden sash around his chest. In Daniel the Messiah is clothed like a priest and in the Revelation like a king. The prophet Zechariah also prophesied of the Savior as both king and priest when he received the vision of the lamp-stand of gold and the seven lamps and of the two olive trees. (Zechariah 4). The angel also told the prophet Zechariah that the two olive trees are two anointed ones, the priest and the king. In the vision the priest Joshua helps rebuild the temple and is crowned as king. (Zechariah chapters 3 and 6). Our Lord is now both king and high priest as taught in the letter written to the Hebrews. He is king as ruler of Israel and all nations and high priest as the one who intercedes for us, who is mediator between God and men.

*

What else does the vision of the Son of Man teach us?

The vision in the Revelation resembles in so many ways the visions given to Daniel. The Son of Man I saw had hairs that were white like wool, like snow. But in the visions given to Daniel this describes God, the Ancient of Days: "Thrones were placed, and the Ancient of Days took his seat; his clothing was white as snow, and the hair of his head like pure wool". (Daniel 7.9). In the vision given to me the voice of the Son of Man is like the roar of many waters; in Daniel his voice sounds like the sound of a multitude. (Daniel 10.6). The prophet Ezekiel also heard the voice of God as the roar of many waters. (Ezekiel 1.24; 43.2).

What is the meaning of the vision of the harvest by the Son of Man with a golden crown on his head and a sharp sickle in his hand?

Yes, I saw a white cloud and seated on the cloud one like a son of man, with a golden crown on his head, and a sharp sickle in his hand. (14.14-20). John the Baptist prepared the coming of the Lord. He was the "voice of one crying in the wilderness: Prepare the way of the Lord" as was written by the prophet Isaiah. (Luke 3.1-6). John came preaching repentance and baptizing for the remission of sins and when the people asked him whether he might be the Messiah he answered them saying, "I baptize you with water, but he who is mightier than I is coming, the strap of whose sandals I am not worthy to untie. He will baptize you with the Holy Spirit and fire. His winnowing fork is in his hand, to clear his threshing floor and to gather the wheat into his barn, but the chaff he will burn with unquenchable fire." (Luke 3.16,17). The work of harvesting given to the Christ and announced by the Baptist ends up with the burning of the chaff with unquenchable fire. This is a picture of divine judgment. The Lord who baptizes in the Spirit is also the one who baptizes in fire. The Lord who blesses and gives life is also the Lord who brings judgment on those who persist in doing evil. The apostle Paul in fact taught the Church in Corinth that they were all one body because all had been baptized or immersed into one Spirit; they were all made to "drink" of one Spirit. Immersion or drinking of one Spirit is figurative language and describes this great gift of the Spirit given through the preaching the Gospel and the response of faith and repentance (1 Corinthians 12.12.13; Titus 3.4-6). As the apostle Peter preached on the day of Pentecost the gift of the Spirit is now offered to all who come to Christ and will come to him in the future: "For the promise if for you and your children and for all who are far off, everyone whom the Lord our God calls to himself" (Acts 2.37-40).

So, I understand that the vision of the harvest by the Son of Man in the Revelation is not new? It is a picture of the work of the Christ from the beginning?

In the Revelation as in the preaching of John the Baptist the work of harvesting accomplished by the Messiah is a work of judgment on those who persecute the people of God and who persist in doing evil. This concerns first the dragon that appears in the Revelation and which is the cause of all the harm done to God's people. This is also about the judgment against the two beasts that arise out of the sea and the earth to which the dragon gives his power and authority, and which persecute God's people. Note that the Son of Man is the Messiah who exercises judgment against the dragon and beasts. This is similar to what the prophet Daniel saw in his visions. The savior of God's people is not a beast but those who are at war against God and his people are acting like beasts. The Son of Man is also the one who gathers the grape harvest of the earth and throws it into the great winepress of the wrath of God. (14.19).

But I read in the Gospels that the harvest of God describes the gathering of the saints. I did not have the impression that the harvest was always judgment.

The Lord's harvest is also a work of separation like any work of harvest as Jesus taught us: "Do you not say, 'There are yet four months, then comes the harvest'? Look, I tell you, lift up your eyes, and see that the fields are white for harvest." (John 4.35). The Lord taught us about this harvest of his people many times as Matthew reminded us saying "The harvest is plentiful, but the laborers are few; therefore, pray earnestly to the Lord of the harvest to send out laborers into his harvest." (Matthew 9.37,38). The last words of the Revelation also describe this great harvest of the saints. This will be the time when the holy city, the new Jerusalem comes down out of heaven prepared as a bride adorned for her husband. This will be the time when "the dwelling place of God is with man. He will dwell with them, and they will be his people, and God himself will be with them as their God. He will wipe away every tear from their eyes, and death shall be no more, neither shall there be mourning, nor crying, nor pain anymore, for the former things have passed away." (21.3).

One thing the Revelation of our Lord teaches us is that before his return, before this coming down from heaven in glory, we are not to expect any kind of perfection or paradisiac condition of humanity or even the Church. As already seen in the letters to the seven churches the people of God will be facing immense challenges but the most important one will be whether or not believers in Christ will remain faithful and practice the teachings of our Lord. This is what Jesus had told us and taught us even on the night he was betrayed to be crucified:

"**21** Whoever has my commandments and keeps them, he it is who loves me. And he who loves me will be loved by my Father, and I will love him and manifest myself to him.". (John 14.21)

*

13 I saw in the night visions, and behold, with the clouds of heaven
 there came one like a son of man,
and he came to the Ancient of Days
 and was presented before him.
14 And to him was given dominion
 and glory and a kingdom,
that all peoples, nations, and languages
 should serve him;
his dominion is an everlasting dominion,
 which shall not pass away,
and his kingdom one
 that shall not be destroyed. (Daniel 7.13,14)

6. THE LAMB

"**6** And between the throne and the four living creatures and among the elders I saw a Lamb standing, as
though it had been slain, with seven horns and
with seven eyes, which are the seven spirits of God
sent out into all the earth. **7** And he went and took the
scroll from the right hand of him who was seated on
the throne." (Revelation 5.6,7)

*

*John, what does the Revelation show us about Jesus as the
lamb?*

I was there at the cross with Mary his mother, her sister and
also Mary the wife of Cleopas and Mary Magdalene. We were
all witnesses when the soldier pierced his side with a spear and
there came out blood and water from his side. He himself had
told us that he would die this way and he was called « the lamb
of God » from the beginning by John the baptizer when he

said: "Behold, the lamb of God, who takes away the sin of the world." (John 1.29).

Had not Jesus told you himself about his coming death at the hands of Gentiles?

Jesus spoke precisely about the Gentiles being involved in his cruel death and this was also taught by our prophets and psalms when they say: "Why do the nations rage, and the peoples plot in vain?" and when they speak of rulers and kings who are at war against God's anointed: "Now therefore, O kings, be wise; be warned, O rulers of the earth." (Psalms 2).

I thought it was your people, the people of Israel, who crucified him?

The Lord announced his cruel death several times during the three years he preached and ministered to the people of Israel. We understood his words only later. When our Lord prophesied of his own death, he made it clear that the decision to put him to death would come from the religious leaders, the scribes and the chief priests. Jesus himself was an Israelite as well as his mother. All of us apostles are of Israel. We and many others were not involved in putting him to death. But our Scriptures also teach us that all men and all peoples have sinned and have separated themselves from our Father in heaven. The prophet Isaiah had already written about the Messiah as one "who was despised and rejected of men, a man of sorrows and acquainted with grief" (Isaiah 53.3). The Scriptures also teach us extensively that when we hurt others, when we mistreat people around us or hate them, we are also hurting our Lord. What happened at the cross was sinful but is only a reflection of what humanity has dealt with since its origins when Cain murdered his brother Abel. The Lord has taught us that murder comes from the heart and it is the heart that needs to change if we want to overcome this great sin of taking another life:

> **21** "You have heard that it was said to those of old, 'You shall not murder; and whoever murders will be liable to judgment.' **22** But I say to you that everyone who is angry with his brother will be liable to judgment; whoever insults his brother will be liable to the council; and whoever says, 'You fool!' will be liable to the hell of fire." (Matthew 5.21-22)

What does the Revelation show us about Jesus as the lamb?

The Revelation tells us that Jesus is the one "who loves us and has freed us from our sins by his blood"; he is also the one to whom is due "glory and dominion forever and ever". The Revelation assures us also that "he is coming with the clouds, and every eye will see him, even those who pierced him, and all the tribes of the earth will wail on account of him." (1.6,7). I saw the Lord as a lamb when I received the revelation of the throne of heaven and the opening of the first six seals by the lamb.

What is the revelation of the throne and the opening of the first six seals?

This is the vision of Revelation that follows the vision of the Son of man who walks among the lampstands which are the seven churches. This vision of the throne starts when I am shown a door opened in heaven and I hear a voice speaking like a trumpet and saying to me: "Come up here and I will show you what must take place after this". I was given a glorious vision of the throne of God showing us that our Lord and God is worthy to receive glory, honor and power. (4.11). This vision shows us the first six seals and continues until the lamb opens the seventh seal. (8.1). In that glorious vision of the throne of God I saw our Lord as a lamb that had been slain and was standing between the throne and the twenty-four elders on thrones around the throne.

John, I remember you also saw at the end of the vision a holy Jerusalem coming down from heaven; a city with twelve gates and the names of the twelve tribes of Israel on those gates. The city had also twelve foundations with the name of the twelve apostles. Was the Lord showing us the same thing with the twenty-four elders seated on thrones around the throne?

Yes, and in the vision of the throne we also have the number of those God has sealed on their foreheads — 144,000 from every tribe of the sons of Israel. To this the vision adds also a great multitude from every nation and from all tribes, peoples and languages and who praise God as well as the lamb saying, "Salvation belongs to our God who sits on the throne and to the lamb." (7.8,9). It is said of them that "they have washed their robes and made them white in the blood of the lamb" (7.14).

I noticed that the lamb is mentioned a number of times in that second great vision given to you of the throne in heaven. He is also called the Lion of the tribe of Judah and the root of David. It also says about him that he is the only one who is found worthy to open up the seals of the scroll in the hand of God.

In the vision the lamb is between the throne and the twenty-four elders. When the lamb is called by the mighty angel as the one who is worthy to open the seals of the scroll he goes to the throne and takes the scroll from the hand of God. (5.7)

Do you mean that the lamb moves to the throne at that point?

Yes, first the vision declares that the lamb, the lion of the tribe of Judah and root of David has conquered so that he can open the scroll and its seven seals. (5.4). The lamb is standing between the throne and four living creatures and the twenty-four elders, but he then moves to the throne to receive the scroll from the Father who is seated on the throne.

And every time it is the lamb who opens the seals?

Yes, that is what the lamb does. So, we see him opening every seal until he opens the seventh seal, and the seven trumpets are given to the seven angels who stand before God. (8.1,2)

What happens to the lamb afterwards?

After the vision of the woman and the dragon and the appearing of the beast from the sea and the beast from the earth, the Revelation shows us the lamb standing on Mount Zion and with him 144,000 who had his name and his Father's name written on their foreheads. (14.1). Later on, the beast with the seven horns and ten heads that carries the prostitute makes war against the lamb, but the Revelation proclaims that the lamb will conquer them for he is Lord of lords and King of kings. (17.9-14). Later in the Revelation we find the blessing given to those who are invited to the marriage supper of the lamb. (19.9) When the holy city comes down from heaven I saw no temple in the city for its temple is the Lord God the Almighty and the lamb. (21.22). The city has no need of sun or moon to shine on it for the glory of God gives its light, and its light is the lamb. (21.22,23). The Revelation showed me that the city has a river of the water of life flowing from the throne of God and of the lamb. (22.1) The throne I saw was the throne of God and of the lamb and his servants worship him. (22.3).

So, if I understand, all along we see the lamb; in the beginning of the Revelation the lamb stands between the throne and the twenty-four elders, but he moves to the throne to receive the scroll which he is worthy to unseal. We then see him sitting on the throne and being worshipped.

That is also what our Gospels as well as our epistles teach. The lamb of God who comes for baptism by John the Baptist and takes away the sin of the world is also the word who was in the beginning, who was with God and was God. (John 1.1). He became flesh and we the apostles saw his glory as of the only Son from the Father, full of grace and truth (John 1.14). From his fulness we have received grace upon grace.

> "**17** For the law was given through Moses; grace and truth came through Jesus Christ. **18** No one has ever seen God; the only God, who is at the Father's side. (John 1.17,18)

No one has ever seen God but the only God who is the Father's side he has made him known (John 1.16-18).

*

> **31** "And taking the twelve, he said to them, 'See, we are going up to Jerusalem, and everything that is written about the Son of Man by the prophets will be accomplished. **32** For he will be delivered over to the Gentiles and will be mocked and shamefully treated and spit upon. **33** And after flogging him, they will kill him, and on the third day he will rise.' **34** But they understood none of these things. This saying was hidden from them, and they did not grasp what was said. (Luke 18.31–34)

7. THE MAJESTY OF THE CHRIST

"**4** After this I looked, and behold, a door standing open in heaven! And the first voice, which I had heard speaking to me like a trumpet, said, "Come up here, and I will show you what must take place after this." **2** At once I was in the Spirit, and behold, a throne stood in heaven, with one seated on the throne. **3** And he who sat there had the appearance of jasper and carnelian, and around the throne was a rainbow that had the appearance of an emerald. (Revelation 4.1-3)

*

John, after you saw the vision of the Christ in the midst of the lampstands you mention that you saw a door standing open in heaven and you heard saying loudly to you "Come up here, and I will show you what must take place after this." (4.1). For many people today in the 21st century the word "heaven" de-scribes the stars, galaxies, black holes and many other things astronomers have observed and studied. Does heaven really exist? Could you help us understand heaven?

Yann, you will notice at the start of this vision that the Lord showed me a door standing open in heaven. (4.1). If you will go back to the prophet Ezekiel who was earlier on in the Baby-lonian captivity you will remember that the same thing hap-pened to him when "by the Chebar canal the heavens were opened" and he saw visions of God. You will also remember that part of this vision and opening of the heavens were words he heard from the Lord, words which we find in the book we call by the name of the prophet Ezekiel — God strengthens. (Ezekiel 1.1-3). God spoke to the prophet Ezekiel and said to him: "Son of man, stand on your feet, and I will speak with you". (Ezekiel 2.1). What this is mainly saying in Ezekiel as well as other prophets and the Revelation is that the visions and words that were given to me were not my own invention or human fables but came from God himself. Heaven, the pres-ence of God, is the source of these visions and words.

But what can we learn about heaven from these visions and words?

The visions given to me from "heaven" are not mainly about "heaven" but about living our lives with humble and repentant hearts. When he showed me the throne in heaven and described the colorful precious stones such as jasper or emerald; when he showed me lightning coming from the throne or a sea of glass like crystal the Lord was giving us a vision, an image of his presence that we could understand. But we should also remem-ber the words of wisdom from our brother and apostle Paul when writing to Timothy about the appearing of our Lord Jesus Christ who is the only Sovereign, the King of kings and Lord of lords, who alone has immortality, who dwells in an unapproachable light whom no one has ever seen or can see. (1 Timothy 6.14-16). He also reminded the brethren in Corinth how he had been caught to the third heaven, not knowing whether or not he was in his body and heard things that cannot be told, which words could not express or describe. (2 Corinthians 12.1-7).

John, there is a lot about heaven in the Revelation, can we talk about it later? I would like to go back to the vision of the throne at the beginning of the visions.

Yes, we can do that. Just let me know when you want to talk about this.

What is special about the vision of the throne?

The vision of the throne is not anything new for us who are from Israel and are acquainted with the writings of our prophets. Prophets like Ezekiel, Isaiah and Daniel also saw visions of the majesty and the reign of our God. The vision of the throne reminds us who is the true ruler of the world. The majesty and rule of our God but also of the Lord Jesus Christ are at the heart of all of the Scriptures. In that sense the vision of the throne is not showing or teaching things completely new that we knew nothing about. We find the majesty and reign of God especially in our Psalms which we call '*teheeleem*' in Hebrew (praises). When the Lord Jesus was standing before Pilate, he reminded the Roman governor of who was the true source of his authority and who was the true ruler of the world. When Pilate said to him, "You will not speak to me? Do you not know that I have authority to release you and authority to crucify you?" Jesus answered him saying, "You would have no authority over me at all unless it had been given you from above." (John 19.10.11).

But John how are we to believe in the majesty and reign of God when the Revelation given to us is so much about pain and suffering, about opposition to God and his people?

Yann, these two things exist together: God's rule and a world full of death, pain and tears. This is exactly the case in fact throughout all of the Scriptures. This is the case until the Lord returns, when He will wipe away every tear from their eyes, and death shall be no more, neither shall there be mourning, nor crying, nor pain anymore, for the former things have passed away. (21.4) When I saw the vision of the door standing open in heaven I was told to "come up here". And at once I was in the Spirit and I saw a throne in heaven with one seated on the throne. (4.1,2). This is the same vision of the throne that I saw in the last vision when earth and sky fled away from the presence of the one on the throne, and no place was found for them. (20.11)

When you saw that earth and sky fled away what does this mean for our physical world? How will it be changed?

Yann, I saw this in the vision. The earth and sky fled away at the presence of the one on the throne. The vision is teaching us that the Lord is exalted over the earth and sky. Nothing escapes his rule. The vision is showing us what the apostle Paul taught us in his letter to the Philippians, that God has highly exalted the name of Jesus and given him a name which is above every name, that at the name of Jesus every knee should bow, of things in heaven and things on earth and under the earth and that every tongue should confess that Jesus Christ is Lord. (Philippians 2.10,11). As we sing in our Psalms the name of the Lord is majestic in all the earth and he has set his glory above the heavens. (Psalm 8.1).

But does Revelation or the Scriptures teach us that there will be a new heaven and a new earth, a renewal of all creation?

God is sovereign over all things, even the sun and stars and all created beings on the earth. This is taught all over the Scriptures. But remember that this world that God created was and is "good". The earth, stars or trees are part of God's good creation of which he has entrusted us the care as he did in the very beginning to Adam and Eve. What we learn from the Scriptures is that our God has a plan to renew all things, including the creation. This is taught also by the apostle Paul in his letter to the Romans. (Romans 8.18-25). As we continue these conversations about the Revelation, we will see how this is also part of God's gracious and loving plan.

As I read the Revelation, I was struck by the royal descriptions of God but also of the Lamb, the King of kings. What can you tell us about this? Where I live there are no kings or emperors; many countries now elect a president and also their leaders and rulers.

When the Lord gave the Revelation, he wanted to give his saints a teaching that would help them understand how God viewed the Roman emperors and leaders. And God has not changed his views of rulers and leaders of nations. It is a teaching that is important for the presidents and rulers your peoples now elect. Your presidents and rulers are different from Nero or Vespasian, but they are still accountable to God especially when it comes to their opposition to Christ or his people. They are accountable to the one who is the judge of all, to the Lord Jesus. Remember the words of Paul as he spoke in Athens: "The times of ignorance God overlooked, but now he commands all peoples everywhere to repent because he has fixed a day on which he will judge the world in righteousness by a man whom he has appointed; and to this he has given assurance to all by raising him from the dead." (Acts 17.30,31) This is what is meant by the name that is written on the Lord has he rides on a white horse: King of kings and Lord of lords. (19.16)

The descriptions in the Revelation of the majesty of Christ, the King of kings are impressive but how are they to be understood in real life, with real people, kings or rulers even today in 2022?

Yann, you ask a very important question, one that has always been in the minds of believers even under the old covenant. Our prophets such as Isaiah, Jeremiah or Daniel received impressive revelations of the glory and majesty of God and His messiah. This is also the case in our Psalms. In regards to this, the Revelation does not present anything new. The Lord gave me his Revelation as I was in exile on the isle of Patmos and remember that I was exiled as a partner in the "Kingdom" and on account of the word of God and the testimony of Jesus. (1.9). Remember the greeting I shared with the churches — greeting of grace and peace "from him who is and who was and who is to come and from the seven spirits who are before his throne". (1.4). The majesty we believe in is the majesty of the one who is "love", the one who is peace and graciousness, who came to live among us as a servant. It is the majesty of the one who washed our feet and taught us saying, "You call me teacher and Lord and you are right for so I am. If then, your Lord and teacher have washed your feet, you also ought to wash one another's feet. For I have given you an example, that you also should do just as I have done to you." (John 13.13-15). You remember how it was difficult for Peter to see his Lord wanting to wash his feet and said, "You shall never wash my feet". (John 13.8)

*Yes, John I do remember this in your own Gospel. I was think-
ing about this recently when a believer told me "I am not here
to serve anybody! I am tired of people wanting me to do this or
that!" And I mentioned to this person this very account and
how Jesus calls us to serve others. She was astonished that as a
believer for many years she had never thought much about this.*

We understood Jesus when he talked about the Kingdom and
the power of God. But it was also very difficult for us to understand Jesus when he acted and spoke like a servant. We were
exactly like this believer you mentioned. It took us a long time
before we saw Jesus as the true suffering servant of the prophet
Isaiah who was also the King of our people and all peoples.
The prophet already taught us that the Messiah would be a servant, one who would have "no form or majesty that we should
look at him and no beauty that we should desire him. He was
despised and rejected by men, a man of sorrows and acquainted
with grief, and as one from whom men hide their faces he was
despised, and we esteemed him not." (Isaiah 53.3,4).

*This seems so different from what we read about throughout the
Revelation.*

It is not really different. The one on the throne and who is
King of kings is also the lamb as in the prophet Isaiah. He is
the "one who loves us and has freed us from our sins by his
blood"; he is also the one "to whom be glory and dominion
forever and ever". (1.5,6). The picture we have in the Revelation of the Messiah, who is King and Lamb is the same as what
we find throughout the Scriptures and in the Gospels.

*In this case is there anything unique or special in the Revela-
tion given to the saints on Patmos?*

The heart of our Lord and even of our God is not a heart full
of pride or arrogance. He is holy and worthy of praise. He is

just in all his dealings with us human beings. So, this heart of the Lord has never changed through time, even when we lived under the first covenant of Moses. But the Revelation was given not only to confirm what we already knew but it was given because of very special circumstances the Church finds itself, growing and spreading throughout the Empire. The Revelation shows us why we have to endure so much from the rulers of Rome and even from the people of the Empire as they see us live our lives so differently from everyone one else. Peter the apostle explained this in his own words when he wrote in his first letter, "For the time that is past suffices for doing what the Gentiles want to do, living in sensuality, passions, drunkenness, orgies, drinking parties, and lawless idolatry. With respect to this they are surprised when you do not join them in the same flood of debauchery, and they malign you; but they will give account to him who is ready to judge the living and the dead." (1 Peter 4. 4,5)

So, Peter is saying that the kind of life and behavior taught by Jesus was difficult to accept for the Gentile world under the Roman empire, even to the point that the Gentiles would persecute the saints.

This teaching of Peter is really nothing new. It is constantly taught in the Torah and by the prophets. God has always asked his people to be distinct, to live holy lives. Remember his words in the book of Leviticus: "Consecrate yourselves therefore, and be holy, for I am holy." (Leviticus 11.44). These are the very words quoted by Peter in his first letter, "As obedient children, do not be conformed to the passions of your former ignorance, but as he who called you is holy, you also be holy in all your conduct, since it is written, 'You shall be holy, for I am holy.'" (1 Peter 1.16).

Does the Revelation show this opposition to the saints because of their lifestyle and pursuit of holiness?

It does but the central message is not about this opposition but about the need for the saints to endure and persist in doing good. This is what the Revelation shows in the beginning about the seven churches of Asia. Victory is promised to each congregation but is only attained through perseverance. The letter to the Hebrews teaches us to continue looking towards the Christ and to accomplish his mission. (Hebrews 12.1,2).

But I have some other questions concerning the kingship of Christ. Today we have believers who do not understand how Jesus could be reigning and be ruler of all things when everything in our world seems to be in turmoil. What do you say about this?

This is precisely a difficulty with which the saints struggled at the time the Lord gave us the Revelation. In fact, the Revelation is all about this. None of the visions reduce the expectation of trials for the saints but none of them reduces the central theme of Christ's lordship. The Revelation is constantly describing these two things together.

But John does the Revelation not show the saints that even though their present trials are real they have a hope, the hope of glory? Is this not what is taught throughout the new covenant and apostolic writings?

That is precisely true. There is a hope, and hope has to do with the future, with what our eyes cannot yet see. But this hope and all of God's promises throughout the Revelation do not mean that God is inactive or unaware of the pains and trials of this world. This hope does not mean that God is absent from our lives or unconcerned for this world or the world of the future.

*

1 The Lord reigns, he is robed in majesty;
    the Lord is robed; he has put on strength as his belt.
Yes, the world is established; it shall never be moved.
2 Your throne is established from of old;
    you are from everlasting.
3 The floods have lifted up, O Lord,
    the floods have lifted up their voice;
    the floods lift up their roaring.
4 Mightier than the thunders of many waters,
    mightier than the waves of the sea,
    the Lord on high is mighty!
5 Your decrees are very trustworthy;
    holiness befits your house,
    O Lord, forevermore. (Psalm 93)

8. A DOOR TO HEAVEN

"After this I looked, and behold, a door standing open in heaven! And the first voice, which I had heard speaking to me like a trumpet, said, "'Come up here, and I will show you what must take place after this.' (Revelation 4.1)

*

John, after the vision of the Son of Man in the middle of the lampstands you looked and saw a door standing open in heaven and you heard a voice like a trumpet. Can you talk to us about what you saw and what this means.

The Revelation was given to me from heaven, from the presence of God. In the book of Ezekiel "the heavens were open" and the prophet saw visions of God. (Ezekiel 1.1). The prophet also said that he was seeing the "appearance of the likeness of the glory of the Lord". (1.28).

This vision of Ezekiel and the vision I was given were an "appearance of the likeness of the glory of the Lord", they describe the likeness of God's glory so that it can be understood and written down. Even as we contemplate the stars and God's great creation, we see something of His glory as our Psalms testify: "The heavens declare the glory of God, and the sky above proclaims his handiwork." (Psalms 19.1) The glory of God is beyond anything we can see or touch as one of our Psalms also says, "Be exalted, O God, above the heavens! Let your glory be over all the earth!" (Psalms 108.25).

When he saw these visions, Ezekiel fell on his face and heard a voice speaking to him. We know from our history and the Scriptures that man cannot see God and live. Moses who asked the Lord to be able to see his glory was told these words: "And he said, 'I will make all my goodness pass before you and will proclaim before you my name 'The Lord.' And I will be gracious to whom I will be gracious and will show mercy on whom I will show mercy. But he said, "you cannot see my face, for man shall not see me and live." And the Lord said, "Behold, there is a place by me where you shall stand on the rock and while my glory passes by, I will put you in a cleft of the rock, and I will cover you with my hand until I have passed by. Then I will take away my hand, and you shall see my back, but my face shall not be seen." (Exodus 33.19-23)

John, you wrote in the beginning of your Gospel that Jesus was the Word, that the Word was God, and the Word became flesh and dwelt among us. You also wrote that "We have seen his glory, glory as of the only Son from the Father, full of grace and truth". Is there a difference with what you apostles saw and what Moses saw at Sinai?

We saw the glory of the only Son in the flesh. The Gospel inspired by the Lord was written to describe this glory of the Son of which we the apostles were witnesses. Remember that when Jesus had changed the water into wine at Cana in Galilee the Gospel says that "he manifested his glory" and that his disciples believed in him. In our Scriptures whenever we see the word "glory" this has to do with the person of God. Only God has glory and is glorious. In the Gospel I also wrote that "no one has ever seen God; the only God who is at the Father's side, he has made him known" (1.18). The Lord Jesus has made God's glory known through his perfect and sinless life, through his love and also through the power displayed in his signs.

Remember how Jesus told Nathanael that he would see "greater things" and added "Truly, truly I say to you, you will see heaven opened, and the angels of God ascending and descending on the Son of Man". (John 1.51).

So, the things that Jesus did were exceptional and unique because they demonstrated a direct link to heaven. Does this mean for example that when Jesus changed the water into wine or multiplied fish and bread to feed multitudes this came directly from heaven?

Yes, these signs of Jesus and even his teachings, in fact his entire person were not earthly. They had their origin in heaven.

You mean for example that Jesus who was born of Mary existed already as the Son of God since he came from heaven?

Yes, and this was also the witness of John the Baptist when he said, "This was he of whom I said, 'He who comes after me ranks before me because he was before me." (John 1.15).

Our God is not a changing God just as heaven remains the same. Even though I am living over two thousand years after the birth of Jesus heaven has not changed, has remained the same.

James wrote these words, "Every good gift and every perfect gift is from above, coming down from the Father of lights, with whom there is no variation or shadow due to change. Of his own will he brought us forth by the word of truth, that we should be a kind of first fruits of his creatures." (James 1.17,18) When Jesus spoke to Nicodemus, he told him these words, "No one has ascended into heaven except he who descended from heaven, the Son of Man". (John 3.13). Nicodemus had recognized that Jesus was a teacher come from God "for no one can do these signs that you do unless God is with him".

Would you include the words of truth in what comes from heaven and has been brought from heaven by Jesus?

That is why Jesus is called the "logos", the Word. The law was given by Moses, but grace and truth came through Jesus Christ. (John 1.17).

What does James mean when he says, "of his own will he brought us forth by the word of truth"?

Speaking to Nicodemus, a ruler of the Jews, Jesus taught him that "unless one is born again, he cannot enter the Kingdom of God" The need for a new birth of water and Spirit was a surprise to Nicodemus. A new birth to enter the Kingdom of God is required by God because the Kingdom of God, the Kingdom of heaven is not earthly and does not obey the same laws as pertain to the natural world. In order to explain this to Nicodemus Jesus said these words: "If I have told you earthly things and you do not believe how can you believe if I tell you heavenly things? No one has ascended into heaven except he who descended from heaven, the Son of Man." (John 3.12,13). So, there is a heavenly realm and there is an earthly realm. This was also the message of John the Baptist when he declared concerning Jesus "he must increase, but I must decrease. He who comes from above is above all. He who is of the earth belongs to the earth and speaks in an earthly way. He who comes from heaven is above all. He bears witness to what he has seen and heard, yet no one receives his testimony. Whoever receives his testimony sets his seal to this, that God is true." (John 3.30-32).

If I understand correctly, the words that you heard, and the vision of the throne were also from heaven; they did not originate from the human mind and are not ideas conceived by human beings.

This was also taught by our brother who wrote the letter to the Hebrews: "See that you do not refuse him who is speaking. For if they did not escape when they refused him who warned them on earth, much less will we escape if we reject him who warns from heaven." (Hebrews 12.25).

*

Remember the parable of the rich fool. (Luke 12.13-21). In this parable the Lord reminded us that the rich fool had no concern for his soul. All he could think about was to store up for himself many goods laid up for many years. The only love and concern he had was for his wealth. James also mentions this in his letter when he mentions those who "heap up treasures" in the last days. (James 5.1-3). Our Lord taught that this has to do with what goes on in the heart of man and not just about material wealth, "For where your treasure is, there your heart will be also". (Matthew 6.19-21)

There is great wisdom in being concerned for our souls and our eternal destiny. As in all of Jesus' teachings there is a difference between being foolish and being wise. This is the way the Lord presented his teachings in his sermon on the mount recorded by Matthew. (Matthew 7.24-27).

Was Jesus saying that if we are concerned about heaven and our love for God and our neighbor that means it is a sin to have wealth? That we should live in poverty? I ask this question because I have often met people who believed that Jesus was opposed to wealth or owning things on this earth?

Seeking first the kingdom of God and his righteousness, seeking to lay up treasures in heaven instead of on this earth is about the disposition of our heart, it is about the greatest commandment of loving God and loving our neighbor as ourselves. The teachings that concern the heart of man when it comes to material possessions were not taught by our Lord only to the rich, but first to us his disciples and all those who wanted to follow the Master. These teachings are not something completely new, something our people Israel had never heard before. They are part of our entire body of Scripture. You find these truths in the sermon on the mount but also in our Proverbs and our Psalms. Jesus did not come to abolish the law and the prophets through his teachings but to help understand them and live by them with godly wisdom. We must also understand that living with godly wisdom focused on heaven and eternal life with God is the fruit of the great gift of the Holy Spirit. Remember that it not us who have loved God first is God who first loved us. "In this the love of God was made manifest among us, that God sent his only Son into the world, so that we might live through him." And "If God so loved us, we ought to love one another". (1 John 4.9,10).

Yes John, as you wrote in your Gospel and your letters, the commandment of love is the greatest one without which even our faith is of no validity.

And it is important to understand that heaven is foremost about God's presence and about love as the supreme goal of the Christian life. This is why the warning to our dear brethren in

Ephesus is so important to remember, "But I have this against you that you have abandoned the love you had at first". (Revelation 2.4).

*

Love is about a "fullness" of understanding, of living out what God always intended for his people. (John 1.16). We all have received grace upon grace. Seeking heaven is not about losing something important in order to gain something "heavenly" in the sense of not being of this earth or something that we cannot even appreciate in this present life. No, heaven is about a new fullness of life already promised and taught through our Scriptures. What our Gospels are saying, and the apostolic writings are saying have to do with how Jesus the Messiah brought eternal teachings to their full meaning and also to their full realization in our lives if we listen and obey the Master.

So, heaven is about the future but also about the present life. The rich fool mentioned in Luke's Gospel was laying up treasures for the future but was not really living in the present. Everything in his life was about something that he would not even be able to hold on to or enjoy. He was not like the blessed man of the first Psalm who lives fully in the present and whose delight is in the Law, who meditates day and night on the Law. He becomes like a tree planted by streams of water and yields a lot of fruit — this is not about some uncertain future, about disdaining this present life on earth in order to gain heaven in the future. This is about living fully the present and bringing good fruit in this life.

It is sometimes difficult for people in 2022 to understand teachings about heaven. They often think of heaven as "pie in the sky", something completely unrelated to our present life. So many are focused on the present life and their present happiness without understanding that the call of the Gospel, the teachings of our Lord, have to do with fullness of life in the present, with abundant life.

*

But still, heaven is a place somewhere that is not on this earth and from where you saw visions and heard words from God?

Yes, that is true. But this heaven is not a place in the sense of having nothing to do with our hearts, with our present love for God or the actions we do every day. This word that came to me from heaven reminds us of the first Psalms about those who meditate and keep God's word and are "blessed". (Revelation 1.3). There is comfort and there are promises in the Revelation, but this is also about the life our brethren are living under persecution while enduring great suffering for their faith. They can and should still live blessed lives — with full joy, a great sense of peace and given to serving God in every way.

As we think about the blessed man of the first Psalm who is like a tree that produces a lot of fruit, let us remember that the fruit of the Spirit is love, peace, joy, peace, patience, kindness, goodness, faithfulness, gentleness and self-control. (Galatians 5.22). All of this is about heaven and comes from heaven, from God.

John, let me ask you a question that is often asked in 2022. We often hear today an objection to this good fruit presented as a fruit of the Spirit. We hear that there are many who have no faith in God and do not seek him but seem to have love, peace, joy and other fruit. We are often told also that many Christians and followers of Jesus do not always show such fruit in their lives.

Yann let me ask you a question based on a text from our brother James. Where do good gifts enjoyed by human beings come from?

I believe they come from God.

James teaches us that "every good gift and every perfect gift is from above, coming down from the Father of lights." (James 1.16) So, the good qualities present in the life of unbelievers are they to be considered as gifts from God or not? If God is the source of every perfect gift, especially love, peace and joy why would we attribute these to the efforts and working of man whom we know to be sinful? If God gives the rain and the sun as a gift upon all human beings why would he not also give other great gifts such as love, joy or peace, such as harvests, children or family?

Do you mean that all people can see blessings from God in their lives, even those who have no faith in him?

All blessings come from God, from heaven as taught in our Torah: God's "holy habitation" is foremost and primarily in heaven: "Look down from Your holy habitation, from heaven, and bless Your people Israel and the land which You have given us, just as You swore to our fathers, 'a land flowing with milk and honey.'" (Deuteronomy 26.15).

This is what the apostles preached when they went to Lystra and the people there wanted to worship them like gods. Remember the words of Paul and Barnabas to these non-believing people:

> "**15** Men, why are you doing these things? We also are
> men, of like nature with you, and we bring you good
> news, that you should turn from these vain things to a
> living God, who made the heaven and the earth and the
> sea and all that is in them. **16** In past generations he al-

lowed all the nations to walk in their own
ways. **17** Yet he did not leave himself without witness,
for he did good by giving you rains from heaven
and fruitful seasons, satisfying your hearts with food
and gladness." (Acts 14.15-17)

*But John, if we teach that even non-believers can do good and
be loving, is this not giving them the impression they are fine
and do not need God or the Gospel?*

They may have that impression. But remember that the apostle Paul writing to the Christians in Rome reminded them that
Gentiles who knew nothing of the law or had no faith in God
could be manifesting great qualities and virtues. This should
not trouble us since God is the final judge and we need not
concern ourselves about assuming responsibilities or carrying
burdens which are not ours but only God's.

> "**14** For when Gentiles, who do not have the law, by
> nature do what the law requires, they are a law to
> themselves, even though they do not have the
> law. **15** They show that the work of the law is written
> on their hearts, while their conscience also bears wit-
> ness, and their conflicting thoughts accuse or even ex-
> cuse them **16** on that day when, according to my
> gospel, God judges the secrets of men by Christ
> Jesus." (Romans 2.14-16)

*What about heaven? Is it a real place and can we meet God
there?*

Our Psalms proclaim that the "Lord *is* in His holy temple,
The Lord's throne *is* in heaven; His eyes behold, His eyelids
test the sons of men." (Psalms 11.4). God is ever present in his

heavenly and holy temple not made with human hands. This was true when there was a tabernacle as in David's time or a temple as with Solomon. Stephen about to be stoned quoted the prophet Isaiah as he preached to those who were about to kill him: "But Solomon built Him a house. However, the Most High does not dwell in temples made with hands, as the prophet says: 'Heaven *is* My throne, and earth *is* My footstool. What house will you build for Me? says the Lord, or what *is* the place of My rest? Has My hand not made all these things?'" (Acts 7.47-50 and Isaiah 66.1).

As with the Revelation given to me on Patmos the decrees and judgments of God did not originate from a mountain or from the tabernacle. And later on, they did not originate from the temple which, in fact, was desecrated by idolatry before and at the time of the captivity. The decrees and judgments of God originated from His "holy temple", from his throne, which is in heaven. It is from there that all divine and final decisions concerning earthly matters come which is what our prophets have taught (Habakkuk 2:20; Micah 1:2.) The will of God is perfectly accomplished in heaven, and the Lord taught us to pray for his will to be accomplished on this earth as well: "Our Father in heaven, hallowed be Your name. Your kingdom come, your will be done on earth as *it is* in heaven." (Matthew 6.9,10)

*

15 As for man, his days are like grass;
    he flourishes like a flower of the field;
16 for the wind passes over it, and it is gone,
    and its place knows it no more.
17 But the steadfast love of the Lord is from everlasting to everlasting on those who fear him,
    and his righteousness to children's children,

18 to those who keep his covenant
and remember to do his commandments.
19 The Lord has established his throne in the heavens,
and his kingdom rules over all.
20 Bless the Lord, O you his angels,
you mighty ones who do his word,
obeying the voice of his word!
21 Bless the Lord, all his hosts,
his ministers, who do his will!
22 Bless the Lord, all his works. (Psalm 103)

9. WORSHIP

8 "And the four living creatures, each of them with six wings, are full of eyes all around and within, and day and night they never cease to say,
'Holy, holy, holy, is the Lord God Almighty,
    who was and is and is to come!'" (Revelation 4.8)

11 "Worthy are you, our Lord and God,
    to receive glory and honor and power,
for you created all things,
    and by your will they existed and were created.
(Revelation 4.11)

*

I noticed that worship occupies an important part of the Revelation following the vision of the throne. This worship in Revelation is in the very presence of God. It reminds me of the words of the Psalmist:

95 Oh come, let us sing to the Lord;
    let us make a joyful noise to the rock of our salvation!
2 Let us come into his presence with thanksgiving;
    let us make a joyful noise to him with songs of praise!
3 For the Lord is a great God,
    and a great King above all gods. (Psalm 95.1-3)

Yes, that is true. But notice that in this Psalm the writer invites the worshippers saying, "Let us come into his presence with thanksgiving". When the faithful Israelite praised God, he believed he was coming in the very presence of God, he trusted in his love and care. He came to God as a father and savior, a rock of refuge: "Be to me a rock of refuge, to which I may continually come" (Psalm 71.3).

And the writer to the Hebrews teaches us how we have entered the presence of the Lord through our High Priest Jesus who "entered once for all into the holy places" (Hebrews 9.11) so that we

> "…now have confidence to enter the holy places by
> the blood of Jesus, by the new and living way that he
> opened for us through the curtain…" (Hebrews
> 10.19,20).

*

I have a question to ask you John, how would you describe the sound of the multitude of angels singing in the vision? What impression did that produce in your heart?

When the door opened in heaven, I heard the voice of my Lord inviting me to

"Come up" and sounding like a trumpet. It was the same voice I heard from the Son of Man as he stood among the lampstands (1.10-13).

So, this voice of the Christ is something quite different from a human voice we are used to since it sounded like a trumpet.

Yes, it reminded me of the words of Jesus when he told us about the resurrection of the dead, saying:

> "**25** Truly, truly, I say to you, an hour is coming, and is now here, when the dead will hear the voice of the Son of God, and those who hear will live. **26** For as the Father has life in himself, so he has granted the Son also to have life in himself." (John 5.25,26)

Did not the apostle Paul speak about a "trumpet" when teaching about the resurrection of the dead?

Yes, in his first letter to the Christians in Thessalonica he wrote saying:

> "**15** For this we declare to you by a word from the Lord, that we who are alive, who are left until the coming of the Lord, will not precede those who have fallen asleep. **16** For the Lord himself will descend from heaven with a cry of command, with the voice of an archangel, and with the sound of the trumpet of God. And the dead in Christ will rise first. **17** Then we who are alive, who are left, will be caught up together with them in the clouds to meet the Lord in the air, and so we will always be with the Lord. **18** Therefore encourage one another with these words." (1 Thessalonians 4.15,18).

So here we have a cry of command as well as the voice of an archangel and the sound of the trumpet of God. We should not forget this because the events described here are not only to be seen, they are full of sounds and music.

Yann, this is true, and in the Revelation, this is a very important part of the visions given by the Lord. We read the words, but we should realize that what I heard was beyond anything any human being has ever heard in beauty and power to touch the heart and the soul of man. It is impossible for me even to have words that can describe the pure beauty of the voices and sounds I heard in the visions.

The Psalms mention so often the joy of praising and singing to the Lord.

In the Psalms we even see how this singing comes directly from our souls: "My lips will shout for joy, when I sing praises to you; my soul also, which you have redeemed." (Psalms 71.23).

Music and Singing are often mentioned in the visions of the Revelation.

This is true Yann and as soon as the lamb goes to the throne and takes the scroll to open the seals the Revelation presents to us three songs. The first song is called "a new song" and praises the lamb who has come to open the seals of the scroll. (5.9,10). I heard this singing coming from the four living creatures and from the twenty-four elders.

Would it be true to say that heaven is full of music, full of delight and joy?

That was certainly part of the visions of the Revelation. But we also know that God is very present and also speaks to our hearts in silence or through a gentle breeze as with the prophet

Elijah. (1 Kings 19.10-18). God's speaking to us is not about making a lot of noise.

In the visions I heard the voice of many angels surrounding the throne and the living creatures and the elders; they numbered myriads of myriads and thousands of thousands, singing with full voice, "Worthy is the Lamb that was slaughtered to receive power and wealth and wisdom and might and honor and glory and blessing!" (5.11,12).

At one point I heard every creature in heaven and on earth and under the earth and in the sea, and all that is in them, singing together: "To the one seated on the throne and to the Lamb be blessing and honor and glory and might forever and ever!" And the four living creatures said, "Amen!" And the elders fell down and worshiped. This was praise and worship both for God and for the Lamb for all creatures. It felt as if the celebration was so great that even heaven could not contain it.

*

The words of the four living creatures of the vision remind me of the vision of Isaiah the prophet in the temple. (4.8)

Isaiah tells us how in the year king Uzziah died he saw the Lord sitting upon a throne, high and lifted up and above him stood the seraphim or "fiery ones". (Isaiah 6.1-3).

Is this word "seraphim" the Hebrew word for "fire"?

The word "*saraph*" means to burn. Fire burns and also purifies. When Isaiah saw the seraphim one of them flew to the prophet having in his hand a "burning coal" with which he touched the mouth of the prophet and said to him, "Your guilt is taken away, and your sin atoned for" (Isaiah 6.6,7)

Why did the Seraph touch the lips of the prophet and why did he say these words?

This is because the prophet when he saw the vision of the throne and the seraphim confessed his sin and the sins of his people saying, ""Woe is me! For I am lost; for I am a man of unclean lips, and I dwell in the midst of a people of unclean lips; for my eyes have seen the King, the Lord of hosts!" (Isaiah 6.5)

The seraphim remind me of the cherubim placed by God at the entrance of the garden of Eden as well as well as two golden figures of the cherubim with their wings stretched over the Mercy Seat on the Ark of the Covenant.

These cherubim were also woven into the veil of the tabernacle which separated the holy place from the holy of holies. The prophet Ezekiel also wrote about God who is enthroned on the cherubim. (Ezekiel 10.1-22).

I noted that the first words of praise or worship found in the Revelation are a declaration of God's holiness: 'Holy, holy, holy, is the Lord God Almighty, who was and is and is to come!'" (Revelation 4.8)

These are also the first words of the seraphim in Isaiah's vision of the throne. Remember also the words of the writer to the Hebrews concerning God's holiness and the importance of offering to God an acceptable worship when we enter his presence:

> "**28** Therefore let us be grateful for receiving a kingdom that cannot be shaken, and thus let us offer to God acceptable worship, with reverence and awe, **29** for our God is a consuming fire." (Hebrews 12.28,29).

God's holiness means that God is separate, apart. He is separate and apart from a fallen world and from sin. There is in him not a trace of anything evil. For example, God cannot lie. (Titus 1.2; Hebrews 6.18). He is three times holy in the declaration of the seraphim and in the Revelation, which means he is completely holy. And it is because of his holiness that he calls his people to also be holy, as in the book of Leviticus:

> "**44** Consecrate yourselves therefore, and be holy, for I am holy. You shall not defile yourselves with any swarming thing that crawls on the ground. **45** For I am the Lord who brought you up out of the land of Egypt to be your God. You shall therefore be holy, for I am holy." (Leviticus 11.44,45).

The same command is given by the apostle Peter writing to Christians:

> **13** "Therefore, preparing your minds for action, and being sober-minded, set your hope fully on the grace that will be brought to you at the revelation of Jesus Christ. **14** As obedient children, do not be conformed to the passions of your former ignorance, **15** but as he who called you is holy, you also be holy in all your conduct, **16** since it is written, "'You shall be holy, for I am holy.'" (1 Peter 1.13-16)

This reminds me of the encounter of Jesus with the woman of Samaria in your Gospel when our Lord taught about worship.

Jesus taught the woman from Samaria about the worship that pleases God. Our Lord often taught us about worship. This teaching is very important for the Churches and for every believer. From the very beginning of the Church on the day of

Pentecost, we see that those who received by faith and repentance the preaching of the Gospel were baptized and added to the Church. We also know that "they devoted themselves to the apostle's teaching and the fellowship, to the breaking of bread and the prayers" (Acts 2.41,42). The Lord himself, on the night that he was betrayed, taught us to break bread and share the fruit of the vine in memory of him:

> **26** "Now as they were eating, Jesus took bread, and after blessing it broke it and gave it to the disciples, and said, 'Take, eat; this is my body.' **27** And he took a cup, and when he had given thanks, he gave it to them, saying, 'Drink of it, all of you, **28** for this is my blood of the covenant, which is poured out for many for the forgiveness of sins. **29** I tell you I will not drink again of this fruit of the vine until that day when I drink it new with you in my Father's kingdom.'" (Matthew 26.26-29).

Can you tell me more about the Lord's teachings on worship when he spoke to the woman from Samaria? (John 4).

Discerning that Jesus was a prophet, the woman from Samaria wanted to know where God should be worshipped. Going back to the Assyrian conquest of the northern tribes and settlers from Assyria within those regions, the people of Samaria believed worship of God should be centered on mount Gerizim where Israel in the past would pronounce the blessings from the law. (Deuteronomy 11.29). But our people centered God's worship in Jerusalem. (Deuteronomy 12.5; Joshua 18.1; 21.41; 2 Samuel 7.10).

Our Lord did not respond by mentioning either Gerizim or Jerusalem as the central place to worship God. Instead, he told the woman that

"**21** The hour is coming when neither on this mountain nor in Jerusalem will you worship the Father. **22** You worship what you do not know; we worship what we know, for salvation is from the Jews. **23** But the hour is coming, and is now here, when the true worshipers will worship the Father in spirit and truth, for the Father is seeking such people to worship him. **24** God is spirit, and those who worship him must worship in spirit and truth." (John 4.21-24)

In this response of Jesus neither Gerizim nor Jerusalem are to be the central place of worship of God. Is this correct?

Yes, so the question would still remain as to "where" God should be worshipped. The answer of our Lord is not about "where" but "how". In other words, for God what matters is "how" we worship him and not where we worship him.

In a way this makes sense since God was already worshipped before the law instituted mount Gerizim as the mountain of blessings and Jerusalem as the mountain for the tabernacle and later the temple.

That is true, however the Lord Jesus does not deny the importance of Jerusalem or of the Jewish history. He even confirms this importance with the words "we worship what we know. for salvation is from the Jews" (John 4.22).

So, the Samaritans were mistaken but so were the Jews who considered the need for one special place to worship God. Why is that?

The Lord's words go beyond the idea of a place to worship God to the importance of "how" people worship God. Whether they worship in one place or another, the important truth about worship is that God must be worshipped "in spirit and in truth".

And "spirit and truth" does not describe a place but the spiritual condition: conviction, love, character and even behavior.

This is because He himself is "spirit": "God is spirit, and those who worship him must worship in spirit and truth". Thus, this is the kind of worship God is seeking. Unlike the idols and false gods made by human beings God is uncreated, he is not made of flesh, he is spirit. God is an eternal spirit who is not bound or limited by time or space. This is what our brother Paul preached to the idol worshippers of Athens, saying:

> "**24** The God who made the world and everything in it, being Lord of heaven and earth, does not live in temples made by man, **25** nor is he served by human hands, as though he needed anything, since he himself gives to all mankind life and breath and everything." (Acts 17.24,25)

In fact, the worship described in the Revelation is in heaven, it is not bound by time and space. The words of the worshippers proclaim this fact: "Holy, holy, holy is the Lord God Almighty, who was and is and is to come" (Revelation 4.8).

Yes, and what we learn from the worship in heaven is how we should worship God, as the one on the throne who was, and is and is to come. It is because of who he is and what he has done that worship is due to him.

So, can we consider the descriptions of worship in Revelation as a lesson for worshippers throughout time and space?

If you look at the vision of the throne in the beginning of the Revelation you see that everything near or around the throne worships the Lord. You see also praise and worship being given to the lamb with seven heads and seven eyes that are the seven spirits of God sent out into all the earth. It is all the earth that is invited to this worship, along with the myriads and myriads of angels. (5.6-14).

I was reading this again and noted that the vision mentions the one on the throne, who is the Father, the Son who is the lamb and the "seven spirits of God" (seven torches of fire and the seven eyes of the lamb, 4.5; 5.6). So, this would be the Father, the Son and the Holy Spirit as mentioned for example in Jesus' great commission prior to his ascension. (Matthew 28.18-20).

Note how in this great commission to evangelize the world the baptism of believers, honor is given to the one name of "the Father, the Son and the Holy Spirit". God is one, has one name, and he is called Father, Son and Spirit. The Lord Jesus is the "word and the word was with God and was God. He was in the beginning with God and all things were made through him so that without him was not anything made that was made." (John 1.1-3).

This is how you begin your Gospel. And under the inspiration of God's Spirit, you write similar words in your letters. The message of the Gospel concerns "the word of life", the eternal life which was with the Father and was made manifest. (1 John 1.1,2).

Yes, and indeed our fellowship is with the Father and with his Son Jesus Christ. (1 John 1.3).

The Son of God has come "and has given us understanding so that we may know him who is true; and we are in him who is true, in his Son Jesus Christ. He is the true God and eternal life." (1 John 5.20,21).

If I understand correctly, the worship of the Church today, should be "in spirit and truth" because of God's nature and character, because of who He is and what he has done and said throughout time and space. And this worship includes our rela-tionship with God as being the Father, the Son and the Holy Spirit.

There is no separation really between worship and the first and greatest commandment also taught in the Law and by our Lord: "Love God with all your heart, and with all your soul and with all your might." (Deuteronomy 6.4; Mark 12.30,31).

It is difficult to imagine worshipping God without love for him or without being attentive and obedient to his Word.

The worship God seeks is one that expresses love and love is not bound by time and space. We love God wherever we are and at all times. We love God in all that we do. We worship our God and our Lord Jesus in all that we do: "**31** So, whether you eat or drink, or whatever you do, do all to the glory of God." (1 Corinthians 10.31). We also are commanded to walk by the Spirit in all that we do: "If we live by the Spirit, let us also keep in step with the Spirit" (Galatians 5.25).

If worship is not bound by time and space what about days like the Sabbath or the Lord's day, the first day of the week?

Our people received the command to rest on the seventh day. This was a day of rest given to us but not given to other peoples. God commanded our people to keep the Sabbath at the time they came out of Egypt. (Exodus 16.4,5, 22-30). The book of Nehemiah reminds us of this:

> "**13** You came down on Mount Sinai and spoke with
> them from heaven and gave them right rules and true
> laws, good statutes and commandments, **14** and you
> made known to them your holy Sabbath and com-
> manded them commandments and statutes and a law
> by Moses your servant." (Nehemiah 9.13,14).

The Sabbaths were given to Israel as a sign between God and his people. (Ezekiel 20.10-12). The Gentiles have not been given the Sabbath. Brothers and sisters in Ephesus and elsewhere celebrate the Lord's resurrection by sharing in the bread and the cup in memory of him on the first day of the week. Jesus rose from the dead on the first day of the week, the day following the seventh and it was on that day that he appeared to us at first. (John 20.19; Luke 24.1; Acts 20.7).

As in the creation account when the light was created by God on the first day, our Lord who is the light of the world came back to life in order to bring light to the world.

Even today our brethren share in the Lord's supper on the first day of the week. They meet together to pray and praise the Lord and also to learn from the Scriptures.

Yes, and this has been the case from the very first day the Gospel was preached by our brother Peter in Jerusalem. (Acts 2).

In what way then are we partakers of the heavenly worship described in the Revelation?

The Church partakes of the heavenly worship because these visions show the Church, show the faithful disciples of our Lord, being part of that worship. This is the meaning of the visions that describe the 144,000 and those from every nation and every tongue. (7.1-17; 14.1-4). We who have been reconciled to God by the blood of our Lord, we have gone through the veil and have access to God, as taught in the letter to the Hebrews. Thus the same letter describes the worship of the Church as partaking in the heavenly worship:

"**22** But you have come to Mount Zion and to the city of the living God, the heavenly Jerusalem, and to innumerable angels in festal gathering, **23** and to the assembly of the firstborn who are enrolled in heaven, and to God, the judge of all, and to the spirits of the righteous made perfect, **24** and to Jesus, the mediator of a new covenant, and to the sprinkled blood that speaks a better word than the blood of Abel." (Hebrews 12.22-24).

10. TRUTH ABOUT RULERS

"**13** He is clothed in a robe dipped in blood, and the name by which he is called is The Word of God. **14** And the armies of heaven, arrayed in fine linen, white and pure, were following him on white horses. **15** From his mouth comes a sharp sword with which to strike down the nations, and he will rule them with a rod of iron. He will tread the winepress of the fury of the wrath of God the Almighty. **16** On his robe and on his thigh, he has a name written, King of kings and Lord of lords." (Revelation 19.13-16)

*

John, today in America we don't have emperors as you have under Rome. So much is different for us these days. Sometimes believers feel at loss to understand how to view government and world rulers. We are sometimes not certain of how to un-

derstand and practice in our lives the Scriptures we read both
in the Old and New Testaments concerning these matters. You
are now an exile on the island of Patmos as a decision of Roman authorities. Paul and even Peter have been put to death
under the rule of Nero. How do we understand statements like
the ones made by Paul or Peter in their writings concerning
submission to earthly authorities? How are these Scriptures
and others to be understood also in the light of the Revelation
the Lord has given you and all the Churches?

Yann let me first say that it is a blessing for believers any-
where and at any time to be able to read and study the Scriptures. As our dear brother Paul taught Timothy all Scripture is
God-breathed and profitable for teaching, reproof, correction
and training of believers. Even as I am still here in Patmos, I
know that the Scriptures are under God's supervision and that
the apostolic writings will be preserved by God's providence
and by good men and women dedicated to that task just as it
happened with our Old Testament Scriptures. The love of God
goes along with the importance given to His teachings handed
down through prophets and apostles chosen by him. I recall the
words of Paul that the giving of the law belongs and was entrusted to our people Israel. (Romans 9.1-5). Scriptures
breathed by God give us both the good news of salvation in
Christ and the teachings to help God's people grow in knowledge and to be equipped for every good work. In my Gospel I
recalled the words of Jesus teaching the Pharisees and scribes
concerning the testimony of Scripture to the Messiah: "You
search the Scriptures because you think that in them you have
eternal life; and it is they that bear witness about me, yet you
refuse to come to me that you may have life." (John 5.39).

So, John is there a difference between what we read about Scripture in Paul's second letter to Timothy and what Jesus says to the Pharisees and scribes?

The difference is in how we understand the purpose of Scripture. In Paul's writing to Timothy, we see Scripture as profitable for teaching, reproof, correction and training in righteousness. When the apostle Paul wrote this, he also added an important statement, "That the man of God may be ready or equipped for every good work". When Jesus spoke to the scribes and Pharisees, he was reminding them that eternal life is not found in only study or understanding of Scriptures but in the Messiah of whom the Scriptures bear witness; that in order to have eternal life one needs to come to Jesus.

You mentioned that in 2022 believers are sometimes not certain of how to understand and practice in their lives the Scriptures they read both in the Old and New Testaments concerning these matters. It is good for believers to better understand God's word as it relates to the question of human authorities and rulers; this will allow believers to better love and serve God and their neighbors. But such teaching is not what constitutes the good news of salvation and forgiveness through our Lord Jesus the Christ.

I remember that Paul wrote to the Church in Corinth about the "gospel he preached" by which they were saved if they held fast to that preaching. He also wrote to these Christians that what he preached to them was "of first importance". (1 Corinthians 15.1-10).

The Church in Corinth had been dividing over many different issues and questions such as who baptized who and which apostle, they thought, was more important, and their unity was in danger. There was pride and a lack of love among these

Christians. They were in a similar condition as the Church in Ephesus, abandoning their "first love".

Let me say in my own words what I think you are saying. The questions I am raising about rulers and how to understand the Scriptures in relation to these questions should be studied and hopefully understood but should not take precedence over the life and teachings of the Christ and his work of salvation through the cross and his resurrection. Is this what you are saying? Is this what we need to understand from Scripture itself?

In my Gospel and even the three other Gospel accounts and my three letters and even in this Revelation the Lord is teaching his people, his Church, how to be rooted in Christ, in the faith, hope and love that spring from his work of salvation. As beautifully written by Paul in his first letter to the Church in Corinth, brothers and sisters need to be always reminded of their need to grow up and not remain children in their faith and understanding. But at the same time here on earth we see dimly as in a mirror, we know in part. If brethren were to be judged by their level of knowledge and understanding there would be no hope for anyone of them. So, we need to hold on to faith, hope and love which will always abide, and never forget that among these three, love is the greatest, the more excellent way. (1 Corinthians 13).

This does not mean the teachings of Scripture should be neglected or not practiced. What we need to realize is that when we do not grow in our knowledge and when we neglect practicing what Scripture is teaching us, we are not strengthened and thus are weaker when it comes to sin and temptation. So, this is not about thinking that we can deliberately disobey or neglect any apostolic teaching. As our brother Luke wrote in his Acts of the apostles the Christians baptized on the day of Pentecost "devoted themselves to the apostles' teaching and the fellow-ship, to the breaking of bread and the prayers." (Acts 2.42).

So, John how can we understand statements like the ones made by Paul or Peter in their writings concerning submission to earthly authorities? How are these Scriptures and others to be understood also in the light of the Revelation the Lord has given you and all the Churches?

Both the apostle Peter and the apostle Paul give teachings about submission to kings and rulers. Remember also the important words of Jesus to Pilate: "You would have no authority over me at all unless it had been given you from above." (John 19.11). Peter teaches about this in his first letter and Paul teaches about this in his letter to the Romans. Peter writes to the brethren saying, "Be subject for the Lord's sake to every human institution, whether it be to the emperor as supreme, or to governors as sent by him to punish those who do evil and to praise those who do good. For this is the will of God, that by doing good you should put to silence the ignorance of foolish people. Live as people who are free, not using your freedom as a cover-up for evil, but living as servants of God. Honor everyone. Love the brotherhood. Fear God. Honor the emperor." (1. Peter 2.13-17). Paul exhorts the brethren in Rome with these words, "Let every person be subject to the governing authorities. For there is no authority except from God, and those that exist have been instituted by God. Therefore, whoever resists the authorities resists what God has appointed, and those who resist will incur judgment." (Romans 13.1,2).

The world would be a worse place to live if there were no authorities to check human sinful behavior; so, the apostle adds these words, "For rulers are not for a terror to good conduct, but to bad. Would you have no fear of the one who is in authority? Then do what is good, and you will receive his approval, for he is God's servant for your good. But if you do wrong, be afraid, for he does not bear the sword in vain. For he is the servant of God, an avenger who carries our God's wrath on the wrongdoer. Therefore, one must be in subjection, not only to avoid God's wrath but also for the sake of conscience. For because of this you also pay taxes, for the authorities are ministers of God, attending to this very thing. Pay to all what is owed of them: taxes to whom taxes are owed, revenue to whom revenue is owed, respect to whom respect is owed, honor to whom honor is owed." (Romans 13.3-7).

Those who ask the question about submission to rulers and honoring the emperor must remember that I John am exiled on the Isle of Patmos because of my preaching and teaching of the Word of God. This is mentioned in the very beginning of the Revelation written and sent to the churches in Asia. I am exiled because the Roman authorities do not want me to preach and teach certain truths such as the worship to one God and not to all the gods of Greece and Rome worshipped by the subjects of Rome. Peter and Paul have been killed in Rome under the rule of Nero because that emperor did not want the truth of the Gospel to be proclaimed in the city of Rome.

So, is this saying that submission to the authorities and rulers does not always mean obedience to them in every area of life, especially of the religious life? The authorities in other words do not have the power to legislate in religious matters, in matters of what is right or wrong.

Submission to authorities does not mean we can worship them, serve them or put or trust in them as if they were "God". We should not confuse what we need to render unto God and our responsibility towards "Caesar" or the rulers and governing bodies. They are not one and the same thing! Remember the words of Jesus himself when faced with the question of paying taxes to the Roman authorities: "Therefore render to Caesar the things that are Caesar's and to God the things that are God's" (Matthew 22.21).

Remember also these were the words of Peter when he was told by the religious authorities in Jerusalem to stop preaching that Jesus rose from the dead: "Whether it is right in the sight of God to listen to you rather than to God, you must judge, for we cannot but speak of what we have seen and heard." (Acts 4.19). Submission is to consider oneself under an authority that we can honor and respect but does not mean obedience in all things ordered by that authority. Peter taught us to honor the emperor who was going to put him to death for being a Christian. Peter honored the emperor but did not obey him in worshipping him or living a pagan life. Paul writing to the Romans also mentions the need to be subject to the governing authorities and those authorities at the time were the rulers in Rome including the emperor. (Romans 13.1-7) Jesus taught our people to listen to those who teach the Torah, including the scribes and Pharisees who were opposing him, "The scribes and the Pharisees sit on Moses' seat, so do and observe whatever they tell you, but not the works they do." (Matthew 23.2,3)

If I understand correctly, submitting to governing authorities does not mean we need to live like they live and to believe what they believe.

This is what it has always meant and is very clear from our Old Testament Scriptures. We see this very clearly for example in the life of Joseph who did not disrespect his masters in Egypt or the Pharaoh but continued to serve and worship God or in the life of Daniel who showed respect for the rulers of Babylon and Persia but did not live as they lived nor believed in or served their pagan gods. This is not difficult to understand when we know that every ruler and every authority is under the supreme rule of God the creator and ultimate legislator. Another example would be Moses who did not obey Pharaoh but obeyed God who ordered him to lead the people out of Egypt. Since there is a limit in human authority there is also a limit as to how much we need to obey human authority. We can honor in fact all men even the worse sinners, show them respect and compassion. This does not mean we are required to live as they do in their sinful ways.

How would the words of our Lord apply today, living in the modern world of Europe or America?

> *"Therefore, render to Caesar the things that are Caesar's and to God the things that are God's" (Matthew 22.21).*

Remember that Jesus was answering a question about whether or not to pay taxes. This was a trap set by some of the religious leaders. (Matthew 22.15-22). In this account given by Matthew it was the Herodians who came to Jesus with this question of tax paying. The Herodians were Jews who believed they should show complete submission to everything having to do with Caesar's authority. If Jesus had taught not to pay taxes due to Caesar he could have been brought to court and accused of sedition which could be punishable by death. But if Jesus favored paying taxes to Caesar, he would have lost popularity with a population heavily taxed by Rome and under continual financial pressure. Matthew tells us that Jesus was "aware of their malice" (Matthew 22.18). This statement reminds us of a similar statement we find in my Gospel:

> "**23** Now when he was in Jerusalem at the Passover Feast, many believed in his name when they saw the

signs that he was doing. **24** But Jesus on his part did not entrust himself to them, because he knew all people **25** and needed no one to bear witness about man, for he himself knew what was in man." (John 2.23-25).

*

Jesus' statement - "Therefore, render to Caesar the things that are Caesar's and to God the things that are God's" – is full of godly wisdom and contains in itself the fundamental principle we need to keep in mind and practice as disciples of our Lord. This statement was given as the enemies of Jesus showed him a "denarius". The Lord asked them a question which they certainly thought would condemn him, "Whose likeness and inscription is this". And they answered "Caesar's". On the "denarius" was an engraving of Caesar with a superscription presenting him as the ruler of the land, including his title and authority. But if men owe taxes or other things to human beings, especially those in authority, they also owe things to their creator, God, whose authority is far above the authority of any man. What we owe to Caesar is actually written on the coin. He is the ruler of the land. That is a responsibility given to him by God since God is no respecter of persons and expects justice from all. (Romans 13.1-7; 2.11; Acts 2.34; 1 Peter 1.17; Colossians 3.25).

This is not as if Caesar or anybody else can just act with cruelty and brutality and is not subsequently under God's judgment. The question of how Caesar or anyone else uses his authority is one that God looks at and judges impartially. Where do we find "written" what we owe to God? Is it on a coin made by human beings? Is it not rather in the Word of God and especially in the commandments and teachings of our Lord Jesus the Christ? Did he not send us with the mission of teaching people from "all nations" — which includes every one of every social status, including kings and leaders — to come to him and to "observe all" that he has taught us? (Matthew 28.18-20). Was it not in the same mission statement that our Lord started by saying, "All authority in heaven and on earth has been given to me"?

We should remember the words of our Lord before Pilate who said, "Do you not know that I have authority to release you and authority to crucify you?": "You would have no authority over me at all unless it had been given you from above." (John 19.11).

In his response Jesus confounds the Herodians who attributed almost divine authority to Caesar who himself in fact often claimed to be a "god" to be worshipped. Any time we look at the picture of a human, like the one on the roman coins, we are being brought back to the fact that this human being was created by God for a purpose much higher than himself or any other human being.

John, I come to you from the 21st century and many years have passed since this statement of Jesus. In America we also pay taxes and as with Rome we have armies and government officials. But it is different with us today because it is the people who choose through representatives who will rule over them. Is this not different from your days?

It is different in some ways but Jesus' teachings is still true for you and those who live in this far distant future. The question for disciples is still, "What do you owe to the leaders of your country or nation?" and "What do you owe to God". Whether or not they are chosen by the people, kings and rulers don't have the authority to change what God has ordained. There is no human authority that is not under the authority of the Creator.

But John in the United States today or other countries we live under laws and principles different from Rome.

Yes, this is true. Under the Roman emperors today we have very little choice. We did not choose these rulers and we did not elect them like it happened in some of the cities of ancient Greece. The Roman law provides very little freedom for a great part of the population which are the slaves living throughout the Empire. In his book of Acts our brother Luke shows how the Church from its beginnings had basically no freedoms either to meet or teach. From what I understand you live in a time of human history when nations have "constitutions", documents that often proclaim freedom to choose or to believe; freedom even to speak and express disagreement with your rulers. This is unheard of for us who live in the Empire.

But Yann, do you think that the freedom you have to choose to believe or not, the freedom to assemble and express your views came out of nowhere? Has Christ ever forced people to believe in Him or follow Him? When many were abandoning him, did he force anybody to follow him?

> " "**66** From this time many of his disciples turned back and no longer followed him. **67** 'You do not want to leave too, do you?' Jesus asked the Twelve. **68** Simon Peter answered him, 'Lord, to whom shall we go? You have the words of eternal life. **69** We have come to believe and to know that you are the Holy One of God.'"
> (John 6.66-69)

So, John does this not imply a difference in how we understand submission to rulers, to laws?

Yes, it does. If your constitutions and laws allow you to worship freely, to express freely your views or disagreements with your rulers this means that you are not acting "against Caesar" when you exercise these freedoms. If the rulers of the United States or other nations act in a way that is contrary to their own laws and principles it is them and not the people who are not submitting to established laws.

In our modern age there have been men we call dictators who have ruled with extreme brutality and even murdering millions. How can we believe we should be in submission to their authority?

Yann, if I understood submission to authorities that way, I would not be an exile on this island of Patmos, far from my loved ones and my brethren. As a disciple of Jesus, I owe to God faithfulness to his commands and also to his mission of preaching the Good News of salvation in Jesus the Christ and the truth from God. Has this changed in the 21st century? This Revelation we are talking about you and I and which you can read so many centuries later deals extensively with this very issue of what we owe to Caesar and what we owe to God.

I and the other apostles were not sent into the world as rebels to topple leaders through violence or disobedience. We were sent into the world as light and salt so that everyone who chooses to follow the Lord Jesus may find hope and may live a righteous life. Salt and light do not need to exercise force. Their very presence changes everything. All we need to do and all disciples in the future need to do is practice the teachings of our Lord such as loving our enemies, blessing them, doing good to them. (Matthew 5.43-48); refusing to insult or despise anybody. (Matthew 5.21,22); rejoicing and being peacemakers in the midst of an unbelieving and cruel world (Matthew 5.9-12).

In this case how is the world ever to be changed? How are unjust and greedy people ever going to stop hurting others?

The Lord teaches us to be light to the world, to be salt to the earth. Are these just words? Do we not believe that when people submit their wills to God and act out of love for each other the world is changed by that behavior? What else can change the world if not each person having a better understanding of the two greatest commandments of love for God and love for our neighbor? Are God's teachings in his Word not given in order for human beings to be able to live with justice and in peace with one another?

What else does the Revelation say about rulers and human authorities?

In the Revelation our Lord reveals to us how God views the persecution of His people by ungodly rulers. This is the case first of all of the pagan rulers of Rome from the emperors down to others subject to them. I am here on Patmos exiled by the Roman authorities who also have the power to bring me back to Ephesus. But the Revelation is not just a description of the opposition to disciples of Jesus or even their murder under Roman. It is a vision of comfort and teaches important truths about what it means to suffer for the Lord. The Revelation teaches us that our faith has to endure the hatred of the world. However, this hatred of the world cannot prevent that world from hearing the good news and will not prevent many in the Empire from coming to God and being added to the Lord's Church. It is important also to consider how the Revelation shows us how Satan, God's adversary, is behind all opposition to the faith; how our struggle is not against flesh and blood but against "the schemes of the devil" as our brother Paul wrote to the church in Ephesus. (Ephesians 6.11)

*

"**15** Then the Pharisees went and plotted how to entangle him in his words. **16** And they sent their disciples to him, along with the Herodians, saying, "Teacher, we know that you are true and teach the way of God truthfully, and you do not care about anyone's opinion, for you are not swayed by appearances. **17** Tell us, then, what you think. Is it lawful to pay taxes to Caesar, or not?" **18** But Jesus, aware of their malice, said, "Why put me to the test, you hypocrites? **19** Show me the coin for the tax." And they brought him a denarius. **20** And Jesus said to them, "Whose likeness and inscription is this?" **21** They said, "Caesar's." Then he said to them, "Therefore render to Caesar the things that are Caesar's, and to God the things that are God's." **22** When they heard it, they marveled. And they left him and went away." (Matthew 22.15-22)

11. SUFFERING AND GOD'S REIGN

"15 Then the seventh angel blew his trumpet, and there were loud voices in heaven, saying, "The kingdom of the world has become the kingdom of our Lord and of his Christ, and he shall reign forever and ever." (Revelation 11.15)

*

I noticed that the seventh trumpet blows and loud voices in heaven declare that the kingdom of the world has become the kingdom of our Lord and of his Christ, that he shall reign forever and ever. (11.15).

Yes, and we hear words of gratefulness to God for his reign. This happens often in the Revelation as for example with the blowing of the seventh trumpet and worship of the twenty-four elders, "We give thanks to you, Lord God Almighty, who is and who was for you have taken your great power and begun to reign."

But in our modern world many are those who doubt the reign of God — even his existence — because of the display of evil and suffering in the world.

God gave our people and all believers the book of Job. This book is an example of how our God wants us to look at human suffering. From the start of Job's story, we see that the book is about how one man remained faithful in his ways and in his words against all odds and in effect all alone.

When reference is made to Job for example by James it is about his "patience", his persistence or we can say "endurance". The example of Job is given by James when he exhorts his brethren to be patient. The exhortation to be patient is repeated, "Be patient, establish your hearts, for the coming of the Lord is at hand". The patience he is talking about is not just patience in the midst of pain, it is especially the patience that is an expression of true "love", since James adds: "Do not grumble against one another, brothers, so that you may not be judged". James repeats himself in the same text by mentioning steadfastness "We consider those blessed who remained steadfast. You have heard of the steadfastness of Job…". (James 5.7-11).

John, I have sometimes the impression that Job was "impatient", he spoke words that I don't equate with patience.
Tell me Yann, what are those words of Job?

For example, in chapter 7 of Job we read of Job speaking in the anguish of his spirit, complaining in the bitterness of his soul. He even says to God "You scare me with dreams, you terrify me with visions". He also said, "I loathe my life: I would not live forever. Leave me alone, for my days are a breath." (Job 7.11-16).

In the same text Job even wonders if he has sinned for God to treat him like this: "If I sin, what do I do to you, you watcher of mankind. Why have you made me your mark? Why have I become a burden to you? Why do you not pardon my transgression and take away my iniquity?" (Job 7.17-21).

So, John, how can I understand what is meant by the patience or endurance of Job?

The answer is also found in our Scriptures. Note that God considered Job as one who spoke "without knowledge", as talk from someone who in fact was mistaken. (Job 38.1). There is nothing sinful at not understanding what is happening to us, at being in grief over our pain and suffering or the loss of loved ones.

Job in his torment remains a humble man and that is something very important for God. He responds to God with humility with the following words: "Behold, I am of small account; what shall I answer you? I lay my hand on my mouth. I have spoken once, and I will not answer; twice, but I will not proceed further." (Job 40.4,5)

Job even expresses "repentance" or rather "sorrow" in the way he spoke realizing that he had not really seen or understood the glory and majesty of God despite all the words coming from his three friends and even the young man Elihu, "I had heard of you by the hearing of the ear, but now my eye sees you; therefore, I despise myself and even repent in dust and ashes". (Job 42.5,6). This sorrow of Job is '*nacham*'; it is not a repentance because of sinfulness but a change of mind which in this case brings comfort, reassures him. It is a change of mind that has come about from not only hearing "God" but "seeing him". This is a sorrow that often our Scriptures speak about when there has been grief (as in Genesis 24.67; 37.35; Judges 2.18).

If that is the case how can we understand that Job is an example of patience for us as stated in the epistle of James?

Yann, Job did not understand what was happening to him. He even wondered if he had sinned and God had not forgiven him; he felt that his life was wasted and wondered why he should continue to live. But in all of this, did he sin against God? The answer from God himself is that God did not consider these words of Job as sinful as the end of the book demonstrates when God speaks to Job's friends.

This conclusion is very important for us as we read James and try and understand how we need to look at our pains. I will remind you of all these words which are found at the end of Job:

> **"7** After the Lord had spoken these words to Job, the Lord said to Eliphaz the Temanite: 'My anger burns against you and against your two friends, **for you have not spoken of me what is right, as my servant Job has. 8** Now therefore take seven bulls and seven rams and go to my servant Job and offer up a burnt offering for yourselves. And my servant Job shall pray for you, for I will accept his prayer not to deal with you according to your folly. For you have not spoken of me what is right, as my servant Job has." **9** So Eliphaz the Temanite and Bildad the Shuhite and Zophar the Naamathite went and did what the Lord had told them, and the Lord accepted Job's prayer." (Job 42.7–9).

John, this is really surprising, especially when I read for example what these three friends say to Job all along the book. They seem to agree with what I believe about God and with what Elihu the younger man says about God; they all extol the greatness of God, his sovereignty and rule.

Yann, that is true. But God says this about them, "You have not spoken of me what is right, as my servant Job has." (Job 42.7). We see that God's "anger" burns against these three men. And earlier on it is Elihu who burns with anger "at Job because he justified himself." The young man's anger is, of course, misdirected since he also accuses Job. God did not see fit to rebuke Elihu the younger man.

Why does God at the end of the book rebuke the three older men and not Elihu? John, maybe God did not see fit to rebuke the young man because all that he said was basically the same as what the older men had said before.

There is no explanation as to why God rebukes the three older men and not the younger man. God will not always explain why he does this or that in the course of history or even in the course of our own lives. Our apostle Paul mentioned this in his letter to the Romans concerning a truth that was difficult to grasp for our people Israel — the relationship of God to Israel and to the Gentiles in his wonderful plan of redemption. (Romans 11.25-33). Paul quotes from Isaiah and the book of Job to confirm this idea of a higher thought or purpose on the part of God: "For who has known the mind of the Lord, or who has been his counselor?" (Isaiah 40.13); "Or who has given a gift to him that he might be repaid?" (Job 41.11). This is tied to the apostle's important statement in Romans 11.25ff, "Lest you be wise in your own sight..." The apostle then confirms the "mystery" of the past that is now revealed and which is part of the New covenant with Israel which is that God in fact has planned the salvation of both Gentiles and Israel through a new covenant based on forgiveness of sins.

Whatever the case, we should not believe it is because the young man was correct in all of his statements. He was really repeating everything the older men had said before despite the fact that only the three older men are considered to have spoken with "folly" and are the subject of God's anger. It should be clear to all that older men bear greater responsibility before God, because of their age and experience in life.

Elihu the young man basically repeats what the older men had said before him. He even says, "For according to the work of man he will repay him, and according to his ways he will make it befall him. Of a truth, God will not do wickedly, and the almighty will not pervert justice." (Job 34.11,12). We also note that anger came from the younger man, the one with little experience of life. The youth are not usually given as examples of wisdom in the Scriptures and anger is not a sign of wisdom either: "The anger of man does not produce the righteousness of God" (James 1.20). There is a difference between the "anger" of God and the "anger" of this young man. He was angry at Job, but this brought no relief and no comfort to Job. Could this be a lesson on misplaced anger? A lesson on the hurt that anger can produce?

This relief came only when God spoke personally to Job. It is only when Job was in humble communication with God that his heart was comforted. It is only when we turn to God, look up to him, worship him and are grateful that peace comes to us as the Psalms so often teach us:

> **1** "I lift up my eyes to the hills.
>   From where does my help come?
> **2** My help comes from the Lord,
>   who made heaven and earth.
> **3** He will not let your foot be moved;
>   he who keeps you will not slumber.

4 Behold, he who keeps Israel
  will neither slumber nor sleep.
5 The Lord is your keeper;
  the Lord is your shade on your right hand.
6 The sun shall not strike you by day,
  nor the moon by night." (Psalm 121)

What is the connection between the sufferings of Job and the Revelation?

Just as Job sought answers in his pain the believers in the Revelation when suffering great persecution seek answers from God. We see them praying and asking this question:

> "**9** When he opened the fifth seal, I saw under the
> altar the souls of those who had been slain for the word
> of God and for the witness they had borne. **10** They
> cried out with a loud voice, "O Sovereign Lord, holy
> and true, how long before you will judge and avenge
> our blood on those who dwell on the earth?" (Revela-
> tion 6.9-10)

The response to the saints from the Sovereign Lord is very important and helps us understand the Revelation from the Lord Jesus:

> "**11** Then they were each given a white robe and told to
> rest a little longer, until the number of their fellow ser-
> vants and their brothers should be complete, who were
> to be killed as they themselves had been." (Revelation
> 6.11)

The response from God consists first in the fact that those who cry out to the Lord are given a white robe, the symbol of purity and of God's acceptance. And they are told that more of them would be killed. They are also told that there is a "complete number of those" which means that God himself knows what is going on and knows exactly who is being persecuted or killed for the faith.

But how could this be of any comfort to the saints? And what does it really mean?

Many of us today who follow the Christ are suffering from growing persecution throughout the Empire. The Revelation is showing us that this will last and why it will last. But it is not just the persecutions that are part of the "great tribulation" we are going through. It is also all of God's judgments brought upon the Empire and the peoples under its control. The seals of Revelation opened by our Lord contain plagues and pains upon a rebellious and evil world. But the saints live in this same world. So they endure also these judgments of God despite the fact that their lives are lived righteously. And the same is true with the trumpets of Revelation and finally the bowls. Progressively the judgments become more severe until the entire Empire and its rule over the world is destroyed.

But why so much ruin and judgment on the Empire and the world? What is the point of this?

Yann, what was the point of the plagues the Lord brought against Egypt at the time of the Exodus?

God wanted Pharaoh to let God's people go.

Yes, God wanted Pharaoh and the rulers of Egypt to listen to Him and let his people go. They finally accepted to let God's people go but not until ten plagues hurt their nation and pride. This is also what we find in the Revelation under the Roman Empire.

How is that comparable?

When the sixth angel blows his trumpet, we see another series of plagues, destruction and wars. Following this we learn the purpose of these plagues: to bring about repentance. We see that these terrible things have not brought repentance to the hearts of the Roman persecutors,

> "**20** The rest of mankind who were not killed by these
> plagues still did not repent of the work of their
> hands; they did not stop worshiping demons, and idols
> of gold, silver, bronze, stone and wood—idols that
> cannot see or hear or walk. **21** Nor did they repent of
> their murders, their magic arts, their sexual
> immorality or their thefts.". (Revelation 9.20-21)

But how could such pain inflicted on this persecuting power and rule and even that world bring about repentance, a change of heart?

The severity of the judgments and plagues brought about in Egypt at the time of the Exodus help us understand the plagues in the Revelation. In the book of Exodus God does not begin with the plagues and pains. He begins by sending Moses and Aaron before Pharaoh and the rulers and magicians of Egypt. God begins with signs of his power and words ordering them to obey his command.

We are under persecution and I am now exiled on Patmos but remember that this has happened because so many throughout the Empire are now coming to the faith, because so many have ceased to worship the pagan gods, have ceased to live according to cruel pagan ways. If you read carefully the Revelation you will see the progression of the plagues which are first written words that the seals unveil; after that trumpets warn the rulers of these coming plagues and finally bowls that contain the terrible plagues actually fall upon the Roman persecuting world as it will always fall upon any persecuting power at war with Christ.

*

I noticed that despite the persecution of the saints and scenes of judgments brought against people the Revelation describes times of gratefulness and praise especially in heaven as in the case of the blowing of the 7th trumpet, just before the appearing of the great dragon.

The pain and suffering of the saints does not take anything away from the Father of lights and from his promises to the faithful, "with whom there is no variation or shadow of change" and from whom comes "every good gift and every perfect gift" as taught by our brother James. (James 1.16).

Do I understand that the blessings and gifts we enjoy in this life all come from God, the Father of lights? On the other hand, God is never the source of evil since he is in fact the Father of lights and as you have written in your first letter that God is light and in him is no darkness at all?

Certainly, Job and sometimes even the prophets could not always understand the sufferings they went through, or even righteous people go through. But they could not attribute evil to God despite the weight of their pain or their desire to understand. They remained believers. Despite their circumstances they did not act as Job's wife who told her husband to curse God and die. Remember the words of the writer to the Hebrews, "Without faith it is impossible to please him, for whosoever would draw near to God must believe that he exists and that he rewards those who seek him." (Hebrews 11.6).

The Great Multitude in White Robes (Revelation 7.9-17)

9 After this I looked, and there before me was a great multitude that no one could count, from every nation, tribe, people and language, standing before the throne and before the Lamb. They were wearing white robes and were holding palm branches in their hands. **10** And they cried out in a loud voice:
"Salvation belongs to our God,
who sits on the throne,
and to the Lamb."
11 All the angels were standing around the throne and around the elders and the four living creatures. They fell down on their faces before the throne and worshiped God, **12** saying:
"Amen!
Praise and glory
and wisdom and thanks and honor
and power and strength
be to our God for ever and ever.
Amen!"
13 Then one of the elders asked me, "These in white robes—who are they, and where did they come from?"
14 I answered, "Sir, you know." And he said, "These are they who have come out of the great tribulation; they have washed their robes and made them white in the blood of the Lamb. **15** Therefore,
"they are before the throne of God
     and serve him day and night in his temple;
and he who sits on the throne
     will shelter them with his presence.
16 'Never again will they hunger;

never again will they thirst.
The sun will not beat down on them,'
  nor any scorching heat.
17 For the Lamb at the center of the throne
  will be their shepherd;
'he will lead them to springs of living water.'
   'And God will wipe away every tear from their eyes.

12. THE GREAT TRIBULATION

"13 Then one of the elders addressed me, saying,
'Who are these, clothed in white robes, and from
where have they come?' **14** I said to him, 'Sir, you
know.' And he said to me, 'These are the ones coming
out of the great tribulation. They have washed their
robes and made them white in the blood of the
Lamb.'" (Revelation 7.13,14)

*John, what is the "great tribulation" in the Revelation of our
Lord Jesus?*

The seals opened by our Lord reveal the times of tribulation
for the saints. We are in those times which have come about
through the work of the great dragon and his allies. This is a
central theme in the Revelation the Lord has given us.

*Do you mean that the "great tribulation" is something our
brothers and sisters are in the midst of while you are here exiled on Patmos?*

The Lord has given us the Revelation to comfort those who
live today under the cruel Roman Empire. Jesus proclaimed

this both at the very beginning as well as the end of the Revelation, "The revelation of Jesus Christ, which God gave him to show to his servants the things that must soon take place." (1.1). "**10** And he said to me, "Do not seal up the words of the prophecy of this book, for the time is near." (1.10).

*I remember reading that the prophet Daniel was told at the end of the prophecy given to him: "Go your way, Daniel, for the words are shut up and sealed until **the time of the end**. Many shall purify themselves and make themselves white and be refined, but the wicked shall act wickedly". (Daniel 12.9,10)*

Daniel was told that the words of the prophecy given to him were to be shut up and sealed "until the time of the end". But the Lord in the Revelation is teaching us that the "time is near" and thus not to seal up the words of the prophecy. In the Revelation, the Lord Jesus is called to open the seals which shows proximity in time — this Revelation is to be known by those who are now living under the Roman persecution and is given to comfort them:

> "**3** Blessed is the one who reads aloud the words of this
> prophecy, and blessed are those who hear, and who
> keep what is written in it, for the time is near." (Reve-
> lation 1.3).

What did the prophecy of Daniel mean by "the time of the end"? Is this about the "time" when our Lord returns?

The "time of the end" mentioned by Daniel is not about the time when our Lord returns as he has promised. In the prophecy given to Daniel we see that it is about a period of time or a time in the history of God's people when "many shall purify and make themselves white and refined" (Daniel 12.10). This promise of purification for God's faithful we find at the end of Daniel is already mentioned in Daniel's prophecy about the "seventy weeks" decreed to "finish the transgression, to put an end to sin, and to atone for iniquity, to bring in everlasting righteousness." This work of purification of sins follows the cutting off of the "anointed" one, the Messiah. And following this work of purification of sins comes one, a prince "who shall destroy the city and the sanctuary". (Daniel 9.24-27).

When the Lord Jesus was among us, he taught us about this destruction of the city and the sanctuary and even reminded us of the words of the prophecy of Daniel, even making it clear to us that this is something his apostles would witness: "So when you see the abomination of desolation spoken by the prophet Daniel, standing in the holy place, then let those who are in Judea flee to the mountains." (Matthew 24.15,21; Daniel 12.1).

But John, how do the words of the Revelation apply to us who live in the future?

This word of "blessing" as in all of our Scriptures is also about all of Jesus' followers who need to remain faithful when under tribulation. It is through "many tribulations" that we are able to enter the eternal Kingdom of God. (Acts 14.22). Tribulation and opposition should not take away our hope: "**12** Rejoice in hope, be patient in tribulation, be constant in prayer." (Romans 12.12)

John, do I understand that the idea of "tribulation" which is found throughout the Scriptures is especially linked in the Revelation to the working of human powers such as the Roman emperors?

Yes, even though this is not a completely new idea. We need to remember that it is those in powerful positions who will reject the Lord's anointed in Psalms 2. The apostle Peter applies this Psalm to the rulers in Jerusalem and the Gentile rulers who wanted to kill the apostles for their witness. (Acts 4.23-31). It was the rulers and those with influence who wanted to crucify Jesus. It is those in power in Rome and throughout the Empire who want to silence our brethren. And in the Revelation, we have the same constant message about what to expect from worldly powers.

There will always be rulers and people in power. How can we then have any hope to live in peace?

Did not the apostle Paul ask us to pray about that very thing in his first letter to Timothy?

> **"1** First of all, then, I urge that supplications, prayers, intercessions, and thanksgivings be made for all people, **2** for kings and all who are in high positions, that we may lead a peaceful and quiet life, godly and dignified in every way. **3** This is good, and it is pleasing in the sight of God our Savior, **4** who desires all people to be saved and to come to the knowledge of the truth."
> (1 Timothy 2.2-4)

Our God desires all people to be saved and come to the knowledge of the truth. Peace and well-being depend on this. The knowledge of the truth is needed for all men, those who are of a humble condition and those who rule.

Living in peace and in a dignified way depends a lot on the leaders or rulers of a nation or city. But it also depends on us, on our prayers and our ability to live at peace with all men as the apostle Paul teaches us in his letter to the Romans,

> **"18** If possible, so far as it depends on you, live peaceably with all. **19** Beloved, never avenge yourselves, but leave it to the wrath of God, for it is written, "Vengeance is mine, I will repay, says the Lord." **20** To the contrary, "if your enemy is hungry,

feed him; if he is thirsty, give him something to drink; for by so doing you will heap burning coals on his head." **21** Do not be overcome by evil, but overcome evil with good." (Romans 12.18-21)

Does the Revelation teach us anything about the period of time immediately preceding the return of our Lord?

The Revelation of our Lord was not given to us in order to speculate or know when our Lord would return. The Lord's rule and sovereignty over peoples and nations is taught throughout the Scriptures, including the Revelation. The Lord's return and judgment of the world is also part of this sovereign rule of God.

His return is certain as well as his bringing about all the godly blessings promised to the faithful. As apostles, including Paul, we have not in our inspired writings given any hint as to the time and circumstances of the Lord's return, the time for judgment and the resurrection of the dead. In fact, quite the opposite is true. The Revelation itself speaks of his coming as one who comes as a thief in the night: "Behold, I am coming like a thief! Blessed is the one who stays awake, keeping his garments on, that he may not go about naked and be seen exposed!" (16.15).

Our brother Paul said the same thing when teaching us about the resurrection of the dead when the Lord returns:

"**14** For since we believe that Jesus died and rose again, even so, through Jesus, God will bring with him those who have fallen asleep. **15** For this we declare to you by a word from the Lord, that we who are alive, who are left until the coming of the Lord, will not precede those who have fallen asleep. **16** For the Lord himself will descend from heaven with a cry of command, with the voice of an archangel, and with the sound of the trumpet of God. And the dead in Christ will rise first. **17** Then we who are alive, who are left, will be caught up together with them in the clouds to meet the Lord in the air, and so we will always be with the Lord. **18** Therefore encourage one another with these words. **5** Now concerning the times and the seasons, brothers, you have no need to have anything written to you. **2** For you yourselves are fully aware that the day of the Lord will come like a thief in the night. **3** While people are saying, "There is peace and security," then sudden destruction will come upon them as labor pains come upon a pregnant woman, and they will not escape." (1 Thessalonians 4.14-5.3).

Paul encouraged Christians in Thessalonica to be "ready" for this return of the Lord "as a thief in the night". A thief does not give signs or warnings of his arrival to steal !

Yes, and how were they to be ready? Was it by knowing the precise time of his return or even certain signs preceding his return? Is that the way they needed to be ready? The Word of God encourages us to remain "awake" to his coming which could happen any time. The apostle Paul taught us to be ready by being "sober, having put on the breastplate of faith and love, and for a helmet the hope of salvation." (1 Thessalonians 5.8).

Our Lord himself taught us to be ready comparing faithful followers to five virgins who are ready for the coming of the bridegroom. As the "bridegroom was delayed" said our Lord these faithful virgins were ready for his coming even in the middle of the night. The Lord was not teaching us that the five virgins would be warned ahead of time when the bridegroom would come but that they were ready for his coming at any hour and thus did not become drowsy and sleep like the other five virgins.

Remember that our brother Paul mentioned the return of the Lord with these words of warning: "Concerning the times and seasons, brothers, you have no need to have anything written to you. For you yourselves are fully aware that the day of the Lord will come like a thief in the night." (1 Thessalonians 5.1)

Today we often hear people teaching that wars and rumors of wars would be a sign of Jesus' return. And the Revelation also has references to wars. How are we to understand this? Are we to believe that the more there will be wars the closer we will be to the Lord's return?

In the Revelation we see wars, but these "wars" describe the forces of evil at war with God or His people. The spiritual war that we are going through is the one that has eternal consequences. It is this war described by the apostle Paul in his letter to the Christians in Ephesus – the war of "principalities and powers" in heavenly places against the faithful of God. (Ephesians 6.16-20)

So how are we to understand wars between nations? Are they not signs given to warn us of the coming of our Lord?

Wars between nations or between people are the outcome of sinfulness, of pride and greed. This is what our Lord taught us in the Sermon on the Mount and the letter of James (James 4.1-10). The first war we read about in the Scriptures is the murder of Abel by his brother Cain. And from that point on war becomes a constant part of human history. Jesus comes to bring peace — peace with God and peace between people. (Romans 5.1-11).

These wars between people and nations show the deeper war in the heart and lives of men, the war against God and his will;

the war of evil against what is good, of lies against truth. It is for this war that Jesus came and taught, died and rose from the dead. Even when men are saying "there is peace and security" (1 Thessalonians 5.3); even when men marry and give in marriage, when they have festive times (Matthew 24.38); even when there is prosperity and when people appear to be happy in their condition — they are still at war with God if their hearts are far from Him and from his will.

13. THE GREAT DRAGON AND THE WOMAN

"**12** And a great sign appeared in heaven: a woman clothed with the sun, with the moon under her feet, and on her head a crown of twelve stars. **2** She was pregnant and was crying out in birth pains and the agony of giving birth. **3** And another sign appeared in heaven: behold, a great red dragon, with seven heads and ten horns, and on his heads seven diadems." (Revelation 12.1-3)

*

John, what would be important for us today in the modern age to understand about Satan, the dragon of the Revelation?

Our Lord taught us how to pray about temptation and evil: "And lead us not into temptation but deliver us from evil" (Matthew 6.13). This shows that the battle with evil and the evil one cannot be won with our own strength, without prayer and the help of God. And our Lord has also provided us ways to be protected from the evil one, the armor of God of which wrote Paul in his letter to the Christians in Ephesus. (Ephesians 6.10-20). It is here that the apostle mentioned the importance of the "shield of faith" with which "we extinguish all the flaming darts of the evil one". (Ephesians 6.16).

Our Scriptures do attribute pain and evil to Satan, as we see for example in the story of Job. A lot of pain and suffering also come from the sin of human beings which they choose to commit. Our brother James also wrote important words about this in his letter to the twelve tribes in the dispersion: "**12** Blessed is the man who remains steadfast under trial, for when he has stood the test he will receive the crown of life, which God has promised to those who love him." (James. 1.12).

But James is writing here about trials, not temptations.

Trials are not necessarily temptations to sin. I am here exiled on Patmos. The saints are enduring trials from opposition; brethren are being slaughtered. And this is why James was writing his letter of exhortations and encouragement, "Count it all joy, my brothers, when you meet trials of various kinds." (James 1.3). This is also why the Lord has given us this Revelation where I saw the saints under the altar praying to God saying, "O Sovereign Lord, holy and true, how long before you will judge and avenge our blood on those who dwell on the earth?". (Revelation 5.10). They are given white robes and told to rest a little longer "until the number of their fellow servants and their brothers should be complete, who were to be killed as they themselves had been."

Does not James also write also about temptation?

Whether they are under trials or temptations to sin the saints need to be awake and remain close to their Lord in order to be strong and resist the evil one. Remember the words of James,

"Therefore, it says: 'God opposes the proud but gives grace to the humble.'

> **7** Submit yourselves therefore to God. Resist the devil, and he will flee from you. **8** Draw near to God, and he will draw near to you. Cleanse your hands, you sinners, and purify your hearts, you double-minded." (James 4.7,8)

We are to remain steadfast under trials and be ready to face temptation. Both of these are important to the life of the saint:

> "**12** Blessed is the man who remains steadfast under trial, for when he has stood the test he will receive the crown of life, which God has promised to those who love him. **13** Let no one say when he is tempted, "I am being tempted by God," for God cannot be tempted with evil, and he himself tempts no one. **14** But each person is tempted when he is lured and enticed by his own desire. **15** Then desire when it has conceived gives birth to sin, and sin when it is fully grown brings forth death." (James 1.12-15)

What I see about the churches at the beginning of Revelation is that they are both under trial and also tempted to abandon their faith. Is that what the Word is teaching us?

Yes, and there is really nothing new to this. Both trials and temptations have their source in the evil one. But the fact that the saints are under trial does not mean they are sinful or tempted to sin. In the Scripture it usually means the opposite.

What do you mean John?

It is when the saints are living a holy life and when they are preaching the truth faithfully to the world that Satan wants to discourage them and stop their message. In the Scriptures this is not a knew teaching specific to the Revelation: it is continually taught. Our Lord himself went through many trials and Satan also wanted him to sin. But we know that our Savior never committed a single sin and that is why he can be our high priest who intercedes for us as taught in the letter to the Hebrews:

> "**14** Since then we have a great high priest who has passed through the heavens, Jesus, the Son of God, let us hold fast our confession. **15** For we do not have a high priest who is unable to sympathize with our weaknesses, but one who in every respect has been tempted as we are, yet without sin. **16** Let us then with confidence draw near to the throne of grace, that we may receive mercy and find grace to help in time of need." (Hebrews 4.14-16)

John, does the Revelation reveal anything concerning the working of the devil and our modern times?

The devil, also called Satan, the adversary of God, is active in bringing trials and also temptations upon the people of God. And when it comes to temptation Satan also uses the evil desires of human beings: "**14** But each person is tempted when he is lured and enticed by his own desire." (James 1.14)

If that is the case, how can we hope to overcome temptation since we are all sinners as you yourself have written in your first letter?

I also wrote that when a Christian commits a sin, he should be willing to confess this sin, trust in the advocacy of his Lord Jesus our mediator and live by keeping his commandments:

"**2** My little children, I am writing these things to you so that you may not sin. But if anyone does sin, we have an advocate with the Father, Jesus Christ the righteous. **2** He is the propitiation for our sins, and not for ours only but also for the sins of the whole world. **3** And by this we know that we have come to know him, if we keep his commandments." (1 John 2.1-3)

Is there something unique about the working of the Satan in the book of Revelation?

There are not any truths concerning Satan that we had not known previously in the Scriptures. The working of Satan to destroy people has always been the same: "Your adversary the devil prowls around like a roaring lion, seeking someone to devour. **9** Resist him, firm in your faith, knowing that the same kinds of suffering are being experienced by your brotherhood throughout the world." (1 Peter 5.8,9).

Who is the woman and who is the child, the dragon wants to destroy and kill in the Revelation? (Revelation chapter 12)

The working of Satan against the child and the woman is what we can expect already from all the prophecies concerning our Lord in the Scriptures given to Israel. Even at the time of the fall of Adam and Eve when they were being cast out of God's presence, he pronounces his curse on the "serpent" who also represents the "dragon" of the Revelation. The woman's offspring would be hurt by the offspring of Satan (those who follow him and listen to him) but would in the end "bruise the head" of Satan. This battle for the life of the woman's offspring (human beings) was won at the cross and through the resurrection of our Lord who conquered death and sin.

"**14** The Lord God said to the serpent,

"Because you have done this,

cursed are you above all livestock

and above all beasts of the field;

on your belly you shall go,

and dust you shall eat

all the days of your life.

15 I will put enmity between you and the woman,

and between your offspring and her offspring;

he shall bruise your head,

and you shall bruise his heel." (Genesis 3.14,15)

Who is the woman clothed with the sun, with the moon under her feet, and on her head a crown of twelve stars? (12.1).

The woman gives birth to the child who is the Christ, the one who must rule all the nations with a rod of iron, as was prophesied long ago in many of our Scriptures: "You shall break them with a rod of iron and dash them in pieces like a potter's vessel" (Psalms 2.9). The Christ, our Lord Jesus, has established a kingdom that will last forever when all other kingdoms will be destroyed, as prophesied by Daniel. (Daniel 2.44,45). Once we know who is the child we understand who is the mother of the child.

Was Mary not the mother of Jesus?

Yes, she was, as well as being a beautiful and humble servant of God whose life was entrusted to me as "mother" when our Lord was on the cross as I recorded in my Gospel. (John 19.25-29). In the Revelation the Lord is not teaching us what we already know concerning Mary, he is describing a woman with a crown of twelve stars on her head. By this we recognize the woman as the bride of God in both Testaments. Note also that this woman is clothed with "light from above" – a light that has its origin in the Creator God – represented by the sun, moon and stars. (Genesis 1.7,14; Job 26.7). The sun, moon and stars are all deities worshipped by the gentiles in the Roman and Greek worlds. These are known as the "gods of the chariot races". Remember the words of our Lord who taught us how "the son of man" is the one who has power over the sun, moon and stars. (Mark 13.24-27). The woman is not threatened by the celestial objects worshipped by the Romans. They are there to add value to her royal status. She has received splendor and glory from the one and only god, the Creator. Is this not also what we read in Psalm 8 about the "son of man"? The prophets spoke the same way of these celestial objects (Isaiah 13.10; 34.4; Joel 2.10; 3.4,20). The "gods" of Rome such as the sun, moon and stars have no power as compared to the one who "comes with great power and glory" with the "angels to gather his elect" (Mark 13.26,27).

The woman has twelve stars on her head which stands for the twelve tribes. Our Lord Jesus was born of this woman, the faithful people of God. The child was caught up to God and his throne which is the ascension of our Lord and sitting to rule at the right hand of God. The woman is always God's people whether under the old covenant of the law or in the new covenant of grace and mercy.

The bride of God in both testaments is the people of God, the faithful under both covenants. The covenant between God and his people is similar to the covenant between a wife and her husband. It is a unique and beautiful relationship of love and faithfulness. Our prophets often describe the beautiful love that existed between Adonai and the people he chose out of Egypt:

> **2** "Go and proclaim in the hearing of Jerusalem: Thus says the Lord,

"I remember the devotion of your youth,
  your love as a bride,
how you followed me in the wilderness,
  in a land not sown.
3 Israel was holy to the Lord,
  the firstfruits of his harvest.
All who ate of it incurred guilt;
  disaster came upon them,
declares the Lord." (Jeremiah 2.2,3)

Was the new covenant not made with the Church, not with Israel?

The new covenant of grace and mercy was not made with Gentiles. It was made with Israel and includes the Gentiles who will choose to enter this covenant. Remember that the new covenant was already promised to Israel. Thus when Jeremiah announces this covenant he does so clearly as referring to those who are descendants of Abraham, not to Gentiles : **31** "Behold, the days are coming, declares the Lord, when I will make a new covenant with the house of Israel and the house of Judah, **32** not like the covenant that I made with their fathers on the day when I took them by the hand to bring them out of the land of Egypt, my covenant that they broke, though I was their husband, declares the Lord." (Jeremiah 31.31.32)

The letter to the Hebrews confirms that this prophecy of the new covenant was established with the faithful of Israel through the priestly mediation of Jesus the Christ.

"6 But as it is, Christ has obtained a ministry that is as much more excellent than the old as the covenant he mediates is better, since it is enacted on better promises. **7** For if that first covenant had been faultless, there would have been no occasion to look for a second.

"8 For he finds fault with them when he says:
"Behold, the days are coming, declares the Lord,
    when I will establish a new covenant with the house
of Israel
    and with the house of Judah,
9 not like the covenant that I made with their fathers
    on the day when I took them by the hand to bring
them out of the land of Egypt.
For they did not continue in my covenant,
    and so I showed no concern for them, declares the
Lord.
10 For this is the covenant that I will make with the
house of Israel
    after those days, declares the Lord:
I will put my laws into their minds,
    and write them on their hearts,
and I will be their God,
    and they shall be my people.
11 And they shall not teach, each one his neighbor
    and each one his brother, saying, 'Know the Lord,'
for they shall all know me,
    from the least of them to the greatest.
12 For I will be merciful toward their iniquities,
    and I will remember their sins no more."
13 In speaking of a new covenant, he makes the first
one obsolete. And what is becoming obsolete and
growing old is ready to vanish away." (Hebrews
8.6-13)

*If the new covenant was made with the faithful of Israel, how
are we to understand the Church? Is the Church not a description of God's relationship with Gentiles?*

Yann, the people of Israel were already called the "church" or "congregation", "assembly" under the covenant of the law. That is why we find the word church (ekklēsia) in the Greek translation of the Old Testament, the Septuagint (our Hebrew word 'qāhāl'). It is used for Israel as they gathered together to appear before God or as a general reference to the people of Israel. We find that throughout the Scriptures. (For example, Exodus 12.6; 16.3).

The new covenant of grace and mercy was made with the faithful of Israel. The apostles and early disciples who followed Jesus from the beginning were all Israelites. The Lord has taught us through the apostles and especially Paul that the plan was God was to bring about his new covenant with Israel through the work of Christ. In his Word the Lord also teaches us that the Gentiles who come to Christ are grafted into Israel in that covenant, even though they do not come from Abraham in a physical way.

Remember that under the first covenant, Gentiles were able to enter into the "congregation" of Israel by circumcision and submission to the law. So, there is nothing surprising with this teaching. Now the Gentiles are able to enter into this new covenant with Israel through their faith in Christ — as written by the apostle Paul:

> "**3** For this reason I, Paul, a prisoner of Christ Jesus on behalf of you Gentiles— **2** assuming that you have heard of the stewardship of God's grace that was given to me for you, **3** how the mystery was made known to me by revelation, as I have written briefly. **4** When you read this, you can perceive my insight into the mystery of Christ, **5** which was not made known to the sons of men in other generations as it has now been revealed to his holy apostles and prophets by the Spirit. **6** This

mystery is that the Gentiles are fellow heirs, members of the same body, and partakers of the promise in Christ Jesus through the gospel." (Ephesians 3.1-6)

In his letter to the Galatians the apostle again describes this adding of the Gentiles to the descendants of Abraham:

"**23** Now before faith came, we were held captive under the law, imprisoned until the coming faith would be revealed. **24** So then, the law was our guardian until Christ came, in order that we might be justified by faith. **25** But now that faith has come, we are no longer under a guardian, **26** for in Christ Jesus you are all sons of God, through faith. **27** For as many of you as were baptized into Christ have put on Christ. **28** There is neither Jew nor Greek, there is neither slave nor free, there is no male and female, for you are all one in Christ Jesus. **29** And if you are Christ's, then you are Abraham's offspring, heirs according to promise." (Galatians 3.23-29)

In his letter to the Christians in Rome the apostle Paul describes this another way by comparing the faithful in Israel such as Abraham, Isaac or Jacob as the roots, as an olive tree planted by God into which the Gentiles were grafted as a "wild olive tree". (Romans 11.11-24).

The Church built by our Lord Jesus comprises all the faithful of God and is the wife of God, or in the words of the apostle Paul the wife of Christ. Thus, the husband must be willing to give his life for his wife just as Christ gave his life for the Church:

"**25** Husbands, love your wives, as Christ loved the church and gave himself up for her." "**28** In the same

way husbands should love their wives as their own
bodies. He who loves his wife loves himself. **29** For no
one ever hated his own flesh, but nourishes and cher-
ishes it, just as Christ does the church." (Ephesians
5.25,28,29)

*Tell me more about the woman being clothed with the sun and
with the moon under her feet?*

The woman receives the light from God and sheds this light
day and night on the world — as the sun and moon did in the
original creation. This woman, the wife of God, the bride of
Christ, is called to be the light of world, as taught by our Lord.
This is the meaning of the lampstands given to each of the sev-
en churches in Asia at the beginning of the Revelation and why
the Christ is standing in the middle of the lampstands because
he is the one who brings this light to the churches:

> "**12** Then I turned to see the voice that was speaking to
> me, and on turning I saw seven golden
> lampstands, **13** and in the midst of the lampstands one
> like a son of man, clothed with a long robe and with a
> golden sash around his chest. **14** The hairs of his head
> were white, like white wool, like snow. His eyes were
> like a flame of fire, **15** his feet were like burnished
> bronze, refined in a furnace, and his voice was like the
> roar of many waters. **16** In his right hand he held seven
> stars, from his mouth came a sharp two-edged sword,
> and his face was like the sun shining in full strength."
> (Revelation 1.12-16).

This "woman" is crowned with glory. That is why God calls his
people a kingdom of priests:

"**5**To him who loves us and has freed us from our sins by his blood **6** and made us a kingdom, priests to his God and Father, to him be glory and dominion forever and ever. Amen. **7** Behold, he is coming with the clouds, and every eye will see him, even those who pierced him, and all tribes of the earth will wail on account of him. Even so. Amen." (Revelation 1.5,6)

This "woman" hated and threatened by the dragon is all of God's people under the new covenant and is today being persecuted under Rome. The saints are being put to death and their prayers are lifted up to God saying:

"**9** When he opened the fifth seal, I saw under the altar the souls of those who had been slain for the word of God and for the witness they had borne. **10** They cried out with a loud voice, "O Sovereign Lord, holy and true, how long before you will judge and avenge our blood on those who dwell on the earth?" **11** Then they were each given a white robe and told to rest a little longer, until the number of their fellow servants and their brothers should be complete, who were to be killed as they themselves had been." (Revelation 6.9-11)

So, the male child of the woman is the Lord Jesus.

Yes, and from the time of his birth until his death on the cross the Lord was threatened by the dragon in every possible way.

And the child being caught up to God and his throne in the ascension is Jesus?

The ascension is the enthronement of Jesus at the right hand of God. These were his last words before sending us to all nations to preach the Gospel, baptize believers and teach the disciples:

> "**16** Now the eleven disciples went to Galilee, to the mountain to which Jesus had directed them. **17** And when they saw him they worshiped him, but some doubted. **18** And Jesus came and said to them, 'All authority in heaven and on earth has been given to me.' (Matthew 28.16-18).

Why does the Revelation show the woman as fleeing into the desert into a place prepared by God in which she is nourished for 1,260 days?

1,260 days is also 42 months and is also three and a half years. (Revelation 11.2; 13.5). Note that 1,260 days is mentioned twice (11:3; 12:6); 42 months is also mentioned twice (11:2; 13:5); a time, times and half a time is mentioned once (12:14). God's people, the Church, finds refuge in the desert where God nourishes and protects her. Remember that God delivered his people from Egypt which he led into the desert (Psalm 74.13; Isaiah 51.9). The people were nourished with the manna sent by God. The woman in the Revelation is in the desert for 1,250 days which are three and a half years. Remember that the prophet Elijah was persecuted and was cared for by God in the desert while the drought was going on in the land under the reign of Ahab (1 Kings 17.1-16; Luke 4.25 ; James 5.17).

John, when do the 1,260 days or 42 months of 3 and a half times start?

They start with the Lord's ascension at the right hand of God "when he was caught up to God and to his throne" (12.5).

And when does this period of 1,260 days end?

This period endures throughout the period of time between the Lord's ascension and his return in glory. This is a period of time also known in our Scriptures as "the last days" – the days that last from the glorification of God's Messiah, his ascension, to his return in glory for the judgment.

(Deuteronomy 4.30; Daniel 8.19; Jeremiah 23.20; 30.24; Acts 2.17; Hebrews 1,2; 9.26; 1 Peter 1.20; 2 Peter 3.3; 1 Timothy 4.1; 2 Timothy 3.1;).

John, do you mean that you and I are living in the "last days" until Jesus returns in glory? Many today believe the "last days" have to do with the times close to Jesus' return in glory.

Yann, "the last days" in the Scriptures endure since our Lord came and ascended unto his throne until he returns to judge the world. Our brethren under the Roman persecution are living in "the last days" and you are living "in the last days" – this special time in history when God has accomplished his plan of salvation for all who will come to Christ. He has already received all power and authority in heaven and on earth. (Matthew 28.18). As our brother Paul wrote to the Church in Corinth, the last enemy to be crushed by his power is death itself: "The last enemy to be destroyed in death". (1 Corinthians 15.25, 26).

John, how can we believe that Christ already reigns when we see all the sin and troubles in our world?

This is why the Lord gave us his Revelation. The entire Revelation is a testimony to the truth that pain and suffering, persecution of God's faithful, do not preclude the reign of Christ for those who submit to that reign.

But many today teach that Christ will reign for a thousand But many today teach that Christ will reign for a thousand years on this earth when he returns. That is what they have read in the Revelation.

> "**6** Blessed and holy is the one who shares in the first
> resurrection! Over such the second death has no power,
> but they will be priests of God and of Christ, and
> they will reign with him for a thousand years." (20.6)

Yann, is the Lord saying here that his reign begins at some point for a thousand years? And is this reign on the earth? Have we not already seen not only in the Revelation but in the entire Scriptures that Christ already reigns?

Does the Revelation not mention that these souls come to life, which is the first resurrection?

This is what the Lord shows us in the vision. Those who have suffered for the testimony of Christ and have not fallen to the worship of the beast come back to life and reign with Christ. But we already know that our Lord is king and reigns since his ascension, since "he was caught up to God and to his throne" (12.5; 5.13). We also know that the saints are already priests and kings by their position in Christ our Lord (1.6). So in this case this is not about the Lord beginning to reign for one thousand years or even the saints beginning to reign for a thousand years. The Lord in this vision of the thousand years is showing his people what he has always promised them as he also does to the churches in Asia:

> "The one who conquers and who keeps my works until
> the end, to him I will give authority over the nations
> And he will rule them with a rod of iron, as when
> earthen pots are broken to pieces, even as I myself
> have received authority from my Father." (Revelation
> 2.26,27).

Yes, that is clear. But who are the saints here in the Revelation? Are they all the saints of all ages?

They are those who have been beheaded for the testimony of God and for the word of God. They are those who have not bowed down to the beast Rome. They are the same faithful ones who earlier in the Revelation cry out to God saying,

"O Sovereign Lord, holy and true, how long before you will judge and avenge our blood on those who dwell on the earth?". (6.10).

But what about all the saints throughout time who are also persecuted for the word of God?

The Revelation shows us that none who have suffered or will suffer for Christ will be forgotten, that all of God's people are known by him as they go through trials. (Revelation 14.1-5; 15.1-4)

14. HEADS AND HORNS

13 And I saw a beast rising out of the sea, with ten
horns and seven heads, with ten diadems on its horns
and blasphemous names on its heads. **2** And the beast
that I saw was like a leopard; its feet were like a bear's,
and its mouth was like a lion's mouth. And to it the
dragon gave his power and his throne and great authority. (Revelation 13.1,2)

*

John, what is this beast coming out of the sea? What is so im-
portant about the sea and what do these horns and heads
mean?

Yann, the beast that comes out of the sea follows the vision
of the Revelation concerning the dragon, the woman and the
male child. And especially it follows the description of the de-
feat of the dragon in his efforts to destroy the woman clothed
with the sun and the child. (Revelation chapter 12).

I remember that the child escapes the efforts of the dragon to destroy him and is caught up to God and to his throne. And also that the woman is able to fly from the dragon and seek refuge in the desert where she is nourished for 1,260 days or a time, times and half a time. I believe the woman is God's people, those who remain faithful to God and the child is the Messiah who is sitting in authority at the right hand of God.

Yes, and after that the dragon is furious with the woman and wants to make war on the rest of her offspring (Revelation 12.17).

So, the woman who had the male child then has other children?

God brings into the Kingdom of his Son many from all nations and tongues described elsewhere in the Revelation. The resurrected Messiah is also described as the firstfruit of many brothers and sisters in the Scriptures. Our brother Paul wrote about this in his first letter to Corinth,

> "**19** If in Christ we have hope in this life only, we are of all people most to be pitied. **20** But in fact Christ has been raised from the dead, the firstfruits of those who have fallen asleep. **21** For as by a man came death, by a man has come also the resurrection of the dead. **22** For as in Adam all die, so also in Christ shall all be made alive. **23** But each in his own order: Christ the firstfruits, then at his coming those who belong to Christ." (1 Corinthians 15.19-23).

Our brother Paul also explained under divine inspiration how the Christ accomplished God's plan to bring to himself the people he foreknew even before the creation of the world and how God predestined them to be conformed to the image of his Son, in order that he might, the Christ, might be the firstborn among many brothers. (Romans 8.29). In the Revelation the rest of the woman's offspring, God's faithful throughout the ages, are also those who keep the commandments of God and hold to the testimony of Jesus, they are the Church of the Lord throughout the ages (Revelation 12.17).

And this is when the Revelation describes the dragon as furious and determined to make war on the rest of her offspring and in the vision, we see him standing on the sand of the sea.

Yes, and it is at the point that I saw in the vision given to me a beast rising out of the sea, with ten horns and seven heads, with ten diadems on its horns and blasphemous names on its heads.

John, why does this beast rise up out of the sea? What is the meaning of this vision?

The dragon stands on the sand of the sea because it is from there that he will be able to make war on the offspring of the woman, the Church of our Lord. The beast that comes out of the sea brings us back to the visions of the prophet Daniel, "7 In the first year of Belshazzar king of Babylon, Daniel saw a dream and visions of his head as he lay in his bed. Then he wrote down the dream and told the sum of the matter. 2 Daniel declared, "I saw in my vision by night, and behold, the four winds of heaven were stirring up the great sea. 3 And four great beasts came up out of the sea, different from one another." (Daniel 7.1.-3). In Daniel and our prophets, the sea in its restless waves and movements describes the movements of the nations in history. This is the case from Isaiah:

"12 Ah, the thunder of many peoples;
    they thunder like the thundering of the sea!
Ah, the roar of nations;
    they roar like the roaring of mighty waters!
13 The nations roar like the roaring of many waters,

but he will rebuke them, and they will flee far away,
chased like chaff on the mountains before the wind
and whirling dust before the storm. (Isaiah 17.12,13)

We know in Daniel what the four beasts coming out of the sea describe. They are the empires of Babylon, the Persians, Greeks and the last Empire of iron mixed with clay, Rome.

These successive empires are described in Daniel's prophecy and point to the history of God's people up to the time when comes the anointed one, the Messiah, who is to "finish the transgression, put an end to sin, atone for the iniquity and bring in everlasting righteousness" (Daniel 9.24). The Revelation reminds us of the prophecy of Daniel and describes how the dragon gives his authority to the beast coming out of the sea, which is the last beast of Daniel.

I remember that the beast of Daniel also has horns of which one has eyes like the eyes of a man and an arrogant mouth. (Daniel 7.8,11).

In the Revelation the same beast that makes war on the saints also is given "a mouth uttering haughty and blasphemous words… blasphemies against God." (Revelation 13.5,6).

In the Revelation we see also that this beast has authority and power over every tribe and people, language and nation. It is even worshipped by all these people. The Gospel has spread through the world and many nations since our Lord gave us his great mission of evangelization. But this Gospel is spreading in our world under the rule of Rome and its emperors. That is why I am presently in exile on Patmos. That is also why our brethren are being warned of growing persecution from the beast and the one uttering blasphemies against God.

What are the ten horns and seven heads in the Revelation?

The ten horns and seven heads of the beast from the sea are explained to us later in the Revelation, when the vision of the great prostitute is given. (Chapter 17). The seven heads are the rulers of Rome and the ten horns are the kings of other peoples who have given their power to Rome and who submit to her. (17.14). At this point an angel told me, "I will tell you the mystery of the woman, and of the beast with seven heads and ten horns that carries her." (17.7) This woman which is described as a prostitute sitting on the beast is drunk with the blood of the saints, the blood of the martyrs of Jesus. (17.6).

So, John this is really the same as we have seen from the start of the Revelation. This is about the suffering saints under the last beast, the last great empire which is Rome.

From the very first words of the Revelation and throughout the vision, this is what our Lord is speaking to His people in these days when Satan is doing all he can to destroy the witness of the truth and the life of Jesus' disciples. (1.9).

So, do you mean that what we read later on about the beast from the sea, the beast from the earth and the great prostitute is all about this great time of persecution under this terrible fourth beast already prophesied by Daniel?

This is what the vision of the great dragon tells us. After the ascension of the Christ the dragon is furious with the woman, God's people also called the Church, and makes war on the rest of her offspring. (12.16). To answer your question about the heads and horns, the Revelation tells us that the seven heads are seven kings and also seven mountains on which the woman is seated. The kings that are ruling now and putting Jesus' disciples to death and destroying their lives are the Caesars and the great city is Rome built on seven hills.

But why does the vision mention that five of the kings or Caesars have fallen, one is and the other has not yet come and when he comes he must remain a little while? (17.10).

This is given to us by the Lord to help us understand what our brethren are to expect from these kings or Caesars. When the Lord gave us the Revelation there had been already five Caesars in Rome. We know their names: Augustus, Tiberius, Caligula, Claudius, and Nero.

This would mean that when the Revelation was given to you it was under the 6th Caesar, the one following Nero?

The Lord gave me the Revelation under Caesar Vespasian. After the suicide of Caesar Nero there was civil war in Rome. So, for example Galba started ruling in Rome with the support of the Praetorian Guard but he was murdered after a few months by Otho. This short period of civil unrest lasted a few months until Vespasian was declared emperor by the Senate and founded the new dynasty of the Flavians under which we are presently living.

And this would mean that after Vespasian there will be a ruler in Rome that would have a short rule and after that one the persecuting "beast" would reappear with a new ruler. (17.11).

This is the beast "that is not and is about to rise from the bottomless pit" (17.8). This is the same beast that rises out of the earth that speaks like a dragon and makes the inhabitants of the earth worship the first beast "whose mortal wound was healed" (13.11,12). The persecuting king that reappears and the beast whose mortal wound is healed are one and the same.

So, the Lord gave this Revelation in part to warn his people that great times of persecution were about to resume through the rulers of Rome, the heads of the beast.

At the beginning of the Revelation the churches in Asia are already warned of great trials coming upon the Church. For example, the Lord speaks to the church in Philadelphia saying,

> "**10** Because you have kept my word about patient endurance, I will keep you from the hour of trial that is coming on the whole world, to try those who dwell on the earth. **11** I am coming soon. Hold fast what you have, so that no one may seize your crown." (3.10,11)

But John, you are now in exile in Patmos. Are not all these emperors persecuting the Christians at this very moment?

My exile on Patmos goes back to the reign of Nero. The Lord has given us this last Revelation of his will while Vespasian is emperor in Rome. The emperor in Rome is presently not persecuting our brethren. Vespasian is a worshipper of the Roman gods and a great believer in the omens, especially those concerning his family and descendants. But he is not seeking to be worshipped as a "god" or to kill those who do not worship as he does.

Thus the "first beast whose mortal wound is healed" describes the former times of persecution, especially under Nero?

Even at the present there are those who actually believe that Nero will be coming back to life. We know that this will not happen because nobody knows the time of the resurrection of the dead. But the persecuting power of Rome manifested in the person of Nero will return and that is what the Lord is warning us in the Revelation. You will even note that the Church in Smyrna which is praised by our Lord is warned about coming persecutions:

> "**10** Do not fear what you are about to suffer. Behold, the devil is about to throw some of you into

prison, that you may be tested, and for ten days you will have tribulation. Be faithful unto death, and I will give you the crown of life. **11** He who has an ear, let him hear what the Spirit says to the churches. The one who conquers will not be hurt by the second death.' (2.10,11)

The Lord also has revealed this fact in the fifth seal:

"**9** When he opened the fifth seal, I saw under the altar the souls of those who had been slain for the word of God and for the witness they had borne. **10** They cried out with a loud voice, "O Sovereign Lord, holy and true, how long before you will judge and avenge our blood on those who dwell on the earth?" **11** Then they were each given a white robe and told to rest a little longer, until the number of their fellow servants and their brothers should be complete, who were to be killed as they themselves had been." (6.9-11)

This is also why the Lord told us at the beginning of the Revelation,

"**3** Blessed is the one who reads aloud the words of this prophecy, and blessed are those who hear, and who keep what is written in it, for the time is near."(1.3)

You mentioned that the ten horns of the beast are kings that receive power with the beast and hand over their power to the beast. Who are those kings? (17.12-14)

Rome continues to conquer a good part of the present world and rulers and expand its presence and authority. This will continue in the future. The persecuting power of Rome will be exercised not only in Rome but throughout the world and through those rulers of other peoples conquered by Rome. Even emperor Vespasian continues to expand the borders of the Empire. We can expect growing persecutions of our brothers and sisters throughout all of these regions. Nobody will be safe, not even those who live far away from Rome.

The Revelation tells us that these rulers submissive to Rome "will make war on the lamb": they are of one mind with the beast. (17.12-14). These are the peoples and nations and languages Rome, the prostitute, is seated on. (17.15). Here the Revelation tells us that the woman on the beast, the prostitute, is "the great city that has dominion over the kings of the earth". (17.18).

What will happen then?

The Revelation tells us that these subjugated nations and rulers will end up hating the prostitute and will devour her flesh and burn her with fire. The beast and the prostitute are destined to fire. The persecuting empire will not last forever. As promised by our Lord, the truth of the Gospel and the Church will not be destroyed (Matthew 16.16-19).

*

VESPASIAN

12.1 In other matters he was unassuming and lenient from the very beginning of his reign until its end, never trying to conceal his former lowly condition, but often even parading it. Indeed, when certain men tried to trace the origin of the Flavian family to the founders of Reate and a companion of Hercules whose tomb still stands on the Via Salaria, he laughed at them for their pains. So far was he from a desire for pomp and show, that on the day of his triumph, he did not hesitate to say: "It serves me right for being such a fool as to want a triumph in my old age, as if it were due to my ancestors or had ever been among my own ambitions." He did not even assume the tribunician power at once nor the title of Father of his Country until late. As for the custom of searching those who came to pay their morning calls, he gave that up before the civil war was over.

16.1 The only thing for which he can fairly be censured was his love of money. For not content with reviving the imposts which had been repealed under Galba, he added new and heavy burdens, increasing the amount of tribute paid by the provinces, in some cases actually doubling it, and quite openly carrying on traffic which would be shameful even for a man in private life; for he would buy up certain commodities merely in order to distribute them at a profit.[1]

NERO AND DOMITIAN

Domitian, having shown great cruelty toward many, and having unjustly put to death no small number of well-born and notable men at Rome, and having without cause exiled and confiscated the property of a great many other illustrious men finally became a successor of Nero in his hatred and enmity toward God. He was in fact the second that stirred up a persecution against us.[2]

---

[1] *The Lives of the Twelves Caesars, Vespasian, Suetonius Tranquillus. Loeb Classical Library, 1914. Public Domain.*
[2] *Eusebius, Ecclesiastical History III.22.1-8.*

With equal arrogance, when he dictated the form of a letter to be used by his procurators, he began it thus: 'Our lord and god commands so and so;' whence it became a rule that no one should style him otherwise either in writing or speaking. He suffered no statues to be erected for him in the Capitol, unless they were of gold and silver, and of a certain weight. He erected so many magnificent gates and arches, surmounted by representations of chariots drawn by four horses, and other triumphal ornaments, in different quarters of the city, that a wag inscribed on one of the arches the Greek word 'ἄρκει'…[strong enough, sufficient][3]

---

[3]*Suetonius, Lives of the Twelve Caesars, Domitian 13.*

15. THE MARK OF THE BEAST

"**11** Then I saw another beast rising out of the earth. It had two horns like a lamb and it spoke like a dragon." (13.11).

"**16** Also it causes all, both small and great, both rich and poor, both free and slave, to be marked on the right hand or the forehead, **17** so that no one can buy or sell unless he has the mark, that is, the name of the beast or the number of its name. **18** This calls for wisdom: let the one who has understanding calculate the number of the beast, for it is the number of a man, and his number is 666." (13.16–18)

"**1** Then I looked, and behold, on Mount Zion stood the Lamb, and with him 144,000 who had his name and his Father's name written on their foreheads." (14.1)

"**4** It is these who have not defiled themselves with women, for they are virgins. It is these who follow the

Lamb wherever he goes. These have been redeemed
from mankind as firstfruits for God and the
Lamb, **5** and in their mouth no lie was found, for they
are blameless." (14.4,5)

*

*John, I understand that the beast from the earth is intimately
connected to the actions of the beast from the sea and also to
the actions of the dragon. I would like to know what is meant
by the mark of this second beast and the number 666 and what
is meant by the seal on the forehead of those who follow the
lamb wherever he goes.*

The dragon is the instigator of everything we see in the
Lord's Revelation given to me on Patmos and to all our
brethren. We understand that behind the beasts and anything
they do are actions of the devil, as taught by our brother Paul in
his letter to the Christians in Ephesus:

> "**10** Finally, be strong in the Lord and in the strength of
> his might. **11** Put on the whole armor of God, that you
> may be able to stand against the schemes of the
> devil. **12** For we do not wrestle against flesh and
> blood, but against the rulers, against the authorities,
> against the cosmic powers over this present darkness,
> against the spiritual forces of evil in the heavenly
> places." (Ephesians 6.10-12).

*So, we can say that the mark given to people by the beast from
the sea is a device of Satan.*

Yes, it is a device of Satan. But what is the meaning of that
device, or its purpose, is what we need to ask ourselves. The
Revelation does not leave us in the dark concerning this ques-

tion. The goal of Satan is that only those with this mark on their right hand or their forehead can buy or sell. What would be the consequence of someone not being able to buy or sell?

I suppose it would be very difficult to survive. How would that person be able to feed his family or himself?
That is the whole point of Satan's stratagem as used by the beast. Remember how the writer to the Hebrews exhorts his brethren and says to them,

> "**3** Consider him who endured from sinners such hostility against himself, so that you may not grow weary or fainthearted. **4** In your struggle against sin you have not yet resisted to the point of shedding your blood." (Hebrews 12.3,4).

Our brethren throughout the Empire are warned about Satan's scheme to impoverish them in order to break their faith and hope. This has already begun in cities like Ephesus or Corinth.

How can the rulers and local authorities do this? Is a mark on the forehead or the right hand enough to prevent people to buy or sell?
The mark on the forehead or on the right hand is figurative language just as the seal on the foreheads of the faithful. This is how some of our prophets such as Ezekiel described how God would recognize his children:

> "**3** Now the glory of the God of Israel had gone up
> from the cherub on which it rested to the threshold of
> the house. And he called to the man clothed in linen,
> who had the writing case at his waist. **4** And
> the Lord said to him, Pass through the city, through
> Jerusalem, and put a mark on the foreheads of the men

who sigh and groan over all the abominations that are
committed in it." (Ezekiel 9.3,4)

*I was also wondering about that since the Scriptures teach us
that the seal given to the faithful is the Holy Spirit.*

  The presence of the Holy Spirit in the believer is the seal by
which God recognizes his children. It is also described as a
guarantee of their inheritance, as taught by our brother Paul in
his letter to the Christians in Ephesus:

> "**11** In him we have obtained an inheritance, having
> been predestined according to the purpose of him who
> works all things according to the counsel of his
> will, **12** so that we who were the first to hope in Christ
> might be to the praise of his glory. **13** In him you also,
> when you heard the word of truth, the gospel of your
> salvation, and believed in him, were sealed with
> the promised Holy Spirit, **14** who is the guarantee of
> our inheritance until we acquire possession of it, to the
> praise of his glory." (Ephesians 1.11-14)

The Holy Spirit that inhabits true believers in Christ describes
their close relationship to God through the Messiah, their status
in his sight, their spiritual renewal by the work of God's grace
in their hearts. (Titus 3.5,6).

  Our brothers and sisters do not have a physical seal on their
foreheads, but the Revelation describes this in the language of
our prophets, with images that speak better than words and that
we can easily remember. Remember that our Lord called Herod
as a fox in order to describe his character. (Luke 13.32).

*Would it be then the case that those who worship the beast from
the earth do not have a physical mark on their right hand or*

forehead? That the meaning of this image is to show their relationship to the beast and the dragon?

Those who receive the mark of the beast are those who worship the beast, who serve the beast and this way are intimately connected to the beast, to its idolatrous and evil works. This mark, this close connection to the beast, allows these people to be able to buy and sell. The Empire can this way punish our brethren by strangling them financially.

It is still difficult to understand how the central powers of Rome could have such an impact on the financial life of people throughout the empire.

Rome does not have to make a lot of efforts for this to happen because the pagan world all around us is already doing this at the local level.

What do you mean by that?

Every town, every household and every trade is under the care and protection of a Greek or Roman deity we also call a patron god or goddess. Worshipping these deities is required of the populations, even of the Christians. So what happens when someone is brought to faith in Christ and cannot worship these local and household gods anymore? They are rejected and persecuted by all the idol worshippers. They are not allowed to buy or sell.

Can you give me examples of these local and household patron gods or goddesses.

When Paul preached in Athens the patron deity of the city was Athena which is still the case today. This has been the case in Athens for over five hundred years with the construction of the altar of *Athena Polias.* The god that protects Sparta and Laconia is Apollo. Even the Olympic games are under the care of

Zeus and Olympia. The patron god of Corinth is Poseidon, the god of the sea. On the island of Rhodes people worship Helios.

When pagans become Christians, they are immediately ostracized and rejected since they no longer worship all these gods and goddesses. This is seen by the local populations and authorities as treason to their local gods and dangerous to their welfare.

*

Today we have those who teach from Revelation and tell us that the mark of the beast is a device we call chip that will be grafted into their bodies in order to control them and even what they sell or buy.

Yann, I would not be surprised that people in power would do this. This is consistent with what powers of the Empire and pagan rulers are doing to our brethren. But there is a difference with what the Lord shows us in the Revelation.

In the Revelation this is not about a physical mark of any kind. This goes back to the imagery of our ancient prophets. Thus, the number 666 is not to be found literally on the right hand or forehead of the worshippers of the beast. What you mention is different. It is everyone getting this "chip" on their bodies. In the Revelation the "mark" is given only to those who willingly worship the beast and serve the beast. The brethren in fact are not marked by the number 666, they are sealed with the Father's name on their foreheads. (14.1). This is even mentioned earlier in the Revelation as the great angel rising from the rising of the sun with the seal of the living God declares these words after the opening of the sixth seal by our Lord, "Do not harm the earth or the sea or the trees, until we have sealed the servants of our God on their foreheads. 4 And I heard the number of the sealed, 144,000, sealed from every tribe of the sons of Israel." (7.3,4) We see in this vision that the totality of God's people is sealed and thus under God's care and protection.

Does this mean that those who put themselves under the protection of the local patron gods and the Empire are thus not under the protection of the Lord?

This is the difference we find between those who worship the beast and those who worship the Lord. The Revelation also describes this worship in many places: "**3** and they were singing a new song before the throne and before the four living creatures and before the elders. No one could learn that song except the 144,000 who had been redeemed from the earth." (14.3; 5.9,10; 11.17,18; 15.3,4; 19.1-3; 6-8).

What is the meaning of the number 666?

Those who are sealed by the Lord have the Father's name on their foreheads. But those who have the mark of the beast have a number which is 666. The Revelation tells us the meaning of this number by saying that it is the number of man. The number is also the "name" of the beast. If we look closely, we see then that there is "the name or number of the beast" for the worshippers of the beast and the "name of the Father" for the worshippers of the Lord. When our Scriptures talk about a "name" this has to do with who the person is, their character and thoughts. The name is the person. The prophet Isaiah prophesied of the name of the Messiah and later on the angel told Mary that the baby "will be called the Son of God". (Isaiah 9.6; Luke 1.35). In the Revelation Jesus has a name "which no one knoweth but he himself" and then reveals to us this name as being "The word of God" (19.6). That "name" is also King of kings and Lord of lords. So this is about who the Lord is and not simply a name given to someone. When we invoke the "name of the Lord" we understand that we invoke the person of the Lord and all he is.

So, what is the name of the beast? What is its main attribute? The answer is that this name is the number 666 which is the number of man or "man's number". Here the Revelation is not saying that this is about a specific man but that the mark is merely human. Those who have the power to persecute our brethren and even kill them, who have the power to prevent them from buying or selling are only human beings. This comes from the creation account where we learn that "man" was created on the 6th day, the day prior to the seventh which is the day of rest. Throughout the Revelation the number seven describes the perfection of God, his revelation and his judgments. There are seven seals, seven trumpets and seven bowls. Our brethren are encouraged to remember that those who are at war with the Christ and are persecuting them are mere human beings who themselves are under God's judgment.

16. ARMAGEDDON

12 The sixth angel poured out his bowl on the great river Euphrates, and its water was dried up, to prepare the way for the kings from the east. **13** And I saw, coming out of the mouth of the dragon and out of the mouth of the beast and out of the mouth of the false prophet, three unclean spirits like frogs. **14** For they are demonic spirits, performing signs, who go abroad to the kings of the whole world, to assemble them for battle on the great day of God the Almighty. **15** ("Behold, I am coming like a thief! Blessed is the one who stays awake, keeping his garments on, that he may not go about naked and be seen exposed!") **16** And they assembled them at the place that in Hebrew is called Armageddon. (Revelation 16.12-16)

*

John, what is the meaning of this Hebrew name Armageddon and why is it mentioned with the drying up of the Euphrates river and the coming of the kings from the east?

The name Armageddon comes from the Hebrew and means "hill of Megiddo" where Israel fought great enemies. (Judges 4.15; 1 Samuel 13.8; 2 Chronicles 35.22). These battles came to represent the battles of a holy nation against enemies of darkness.

This name Armageddon is used in the Revelation only one time at the pouring of the sixth bowl. It is not a name that is repeated and explained in the Revelation in so many words. We have to remember that the sixth bowl and the battle mentioned here are a continuation of the vision of the great dragon and his anger against God's people, the woman with the crown of twelve stars. Remember that when the dragon wants to destroy the woman, she is able to flee in the wilderness and remains under God's protection. (12.13,14). The dragon tries to sweep the woman away with a flood, but the earth opens up her mouth and swallows the river meant to destroy the woman. At this point the dragon is furious and "makes war on the rest of her offspring, on those who keep the commandments of God and hold to the testimony of Jesus." (12.15,16). In this figure of speech, the earth swallowed up the river that was meant to destroy the woman. With the pouring of the sixth bowl the river Euphrates is dried up to open the way to the kings from the east. But we are still here with the evil done by the powerful and ruthless beast with its heads and horns. The words coming out of the beast and the false prophet are spoken under the influence of the dragon and demonic spirits. (16.14). The beast in the sixth bowl is still the great empire that persecutes our brothers and sisters and is at war with the Christ. The woman is still the great city that has dominion over the kings of the earth. (17.18)

Is this battle not also mentioned towards the end of the Revelation when Satan is released from his prison after the thousand years reign?

In this later description of the armies of Gog and Magog the Revelation does not mention any more the hill of Megiddo but instead the battle is against "the camp of the saints" also called "the beloved city". (20.7-10). Here the armies against the camp of the saints are in fact consumed by fire from heaven. We see this happening with other examples in the history of Israel, as with Sodom and Gomorrah or in the time of Elijah. (Genesis 19.24; 1 Kings 18.38). This is something my brother James and I had remembered from the Scriptures. We even asked the Lord to bring down fire from heaven upon the Samaritans who would not show hospitality to Him. But he then taught us that the Son of man is not come to destroy men's lives but to save them. (Luke 9.52-54).

I have had some of my friends tell me they did not understand how in the Revelation fire could be brought against people since this was the teaching of our Lord.

The salvation brought by our Lord to humankind is the Good news we need to preach to all nations. This does not mean that the sovereign Lord who is the "judge of all" does not also bring judgment upon evil doers. (Psalm 75.7). Even our Lord himself preached the need for all to come to faith and repentance and to abandon evil ways and sin because of a coming judgment. (John 3.35,36; Luke 13.3). The trumpets in the Revelation are all warnings of God's coming judgment. These trumpets or warnings are given by God so that men would repent. And in the Revelation the Lord shows that despite all the warnings given by the Lord, many refuse to return to him. (Revelation 9.20,21).

Our brother Peter wrote that the Lord is not wishing that any should perish but wants all to repent and come to him:

> "**9** The Lord is not slow to fulfill his promise as some count slowness, but is patient toward you, not wishing that any should perish, but that all should reach repentance. **10** But the day of the Lord will come like a thief, and then the heavens will pass away with a roar, and the heavenly bodies will be burned up and dissolved, and the earth and the works that are done on it will be exposed." (2 Peter 3.8-10).

Many today have spoken and written about Armageddon and believe that this is talking about nations and peoples from the far east, what we call today China and maybe even Russia. Is this what is meant by these images?

Do we ever see in Scripture rivers opening up for the enemies of God's people? Is not this miracle always destined for those who battle on God's side? And is it not clear that the kings from the east are coming to battle "the kings of the whole world" who are acting under the influence of demonic spirits? If the kings from the east are enemies of God how is it that they are coming to make war at Armageddon with these armies under the influence of the devil and led by the kings of the whole earth? And how could all these armies hold in the valley of Megiddo? How would the Euphrates be an obstacle for these armies coming from the far East?

But there are many today who believe that there will be war at Megiddo against the nation of Israel and led by these armies from the far east.

The war we find in the Revelation is not against our nation Israel but against those who "keep the commandments of God and hold to the testimony of Jesus" (12.17). The enemies of God in the Revelation make war against the "camp of the saints" and "the beloved city". The camp of the saints is the same as "the beloved city" and describes the city our brother Paul wrote about in his letter to the Christians in Galatia.

What city is that?

The apostle Paul explains to us the difference between "the present Jerusalem" and the "Jerusalem from above". (Galatians 4.21-30). The "present Jerusalem" which is the city in Israel by that name is the physical city we find in our history and in the land of Israel. The "Jerusalem from above" is the one the Revelation describes towards the end of these visions. Does anyone think that being a citizen of the earthly Jerusalem provides any kind of safety when it comes to God's judgments or the need to repent? Did not the apostle Paul teach us that our citizenship is from above and not from this earth?

> "**20** But our citizenship is in heaven. And we eagerly await a Savior from there, the Lord Jesus Christ, **21** who, by the power that enables him to bring everything under his control, will transform our lowly bodies so that they will be like his glorious body." (Philippians 3.20,21 - NIV).

Was this not also the teaching of the inspired writer of the letter to the Hebrews?

> "**22** But you have come to Mount Zion and to the city of the living God, the heavenly Jerusalem, and to innumerable angels in festal gathering, **23** and to the assembly of the firstborn who are enrolled in heaven, and

179

to God, the judge of all, and to the spirits of the righteous made perfect, **24** and to Jesus, the mediator of a
new covenant, and to the sprinkled blood that speaks a
better word than the blood of Abel." (Hebrews
12.22-24)

*But don't we see constant threats to the nation of Israel today
and even against the Jewish people throughout history?*

The constant threats against Israel or against any other people or nation are not according to God's will. An unbelieving
world is bent against Israel because our people are a testimony
to the world and throughout human history of God's plan to
bless the faithful. Israel has given to us the Scriptures whether
of the old covenant or the new for the most part. (Romans
9.1-5). Our Lord came from the royal tribe of Judah and taught
that "salvation is from the Jews". (John 4.22). Gentiles who
come to Christ are like a wild olive tree that God has grafted
into Israel, the cultivated olive tree. (Romans 11.11-24). At the
same time in Christ all are children of God by their faith. Our
brother Paul wrote to the Christians in Galatia that those who
are baptized into Christ have put on Christ and now "there is
neither Jew nor Greek". He also writes that "If you are Christ's
then you are Abraham's offspring, heirs according to promise"
(Galatians 3.25-29).

*So is the battle of Armageddon a figure of speech, a way for the
Lord to describe to us the spiritual battle described elsewhere
in the Scriptures?*

The dragon is a figure of speech. So is the beast with horns
and heads. Why would it be different for this reference to the
hill of Megiddo and the battle with the kings of the earth?

*Does the Revelation prophesy about events to come and signs
we need to understand concerning the Lord's return in glory?*

Yes, that is true. But the Revelation does this with images and figures of speech coming from the Scriptures. When we understand how God has spoken to us through the examples of Israel's history and the Scripture, we can understand the Revelation. Our brother Paul taught the Church in Ephesus in one of his letters and made it clear that we are not battling with "flesh and blood" but with spiritual forces in the heavenly places.

The Revelation is all about this spiritual battle and the working of the devil throughout the world. So, we need to remember the words of the apostle Paul to our brethren in Ephesus as we teach or preach about the Revelation,

"**10** Finally, be strong in the Lord and in the strength of his might. **11** Put on the whole armor of God, that you may be able to stand against the schemes of the devil. **12** For we do not wrestle against flesh and blood, but against the rulers, against the authorities, against the cosmic powers over this present darkness, against the spiritual forces of evil in the heavenly places. **13** Therefore take up the whole armor of God, that you may be able to withstand in the evil day, and having done all, to stand firm." (Ephesians 6.10-13)

I go back to the battle of Armageddon. If this is a figure of speech, what is the meaning of the drying up of the Euphrates and the kings from the east coming against the "demonic spirits" and kings of the earth gathered at Armageddon? (16.12-16)

Whenever waters are dried up in our Scriptures this always represents or describes God's miraculous deliverance in favor of his people or his servants. First, remember that in the Revelation and before the battle of Armageddon the river poured out of the mouth of the serpent is meant to drown God's people but is "dried up" so that God's people is delivered. (12.13-17). Note also that in the sixth trumpet the Euphrates is the place from which God brings forces against his enemies. (9.13-19). The kings raised by God to the battle of Armageddon come from the east like the angel that appears after the sixth seal and who comes from "the rising of the sun" (7.1-4) to proclaim protection on the people of God, the 144,000. The east or "rising of the sun" is the place of light and hope. Only God, the creator, has the power to dry up the rivers and seas in order to deliver his people. (Psalms 66.5,6; 106.9; 114.3). This is what God did for his people in the opening of the Red Sea and the Jordan river. Isaiah reminded Israel of this miracle when he said:

"Awake, awake, put on strength,
     O arm of the Lord;
awake, as in days of old,
     the generations of long ago.
Was it not you who cut Rahab in pieces,
     who pierced the dragon?
10 Was it not you who dried up the sea,
     the waters of the great deep,
who made the depths of the sea a way
     for the redeemed to pass over? (Isaiah 51.9,10. See
also Exodus 14.21,22; Joshua 3.17; 2 Kings 2.7-14)

Is this also what the prophet Isaiah spoke about when he prophesied of the branch, the Messiah who would come to deliver God's people?
   Yes, this is also what Isaiah prophesied in these words,

"There shall come forth a shoot from the stump
of Jesse,
     and a branch from his roots shall bear fruit.

2 And the Spirit of the Lord shall rest upon him,
   the Spirit of wisdom and understanding,
   the Spirit of counsel and might,
   the Spirit of knowledge and the fear of the Lord.
3 And his delight shall be in the fear of the Lord.(Isaiah 11.1-3)

"15 And the Lord will utterly destroy
   the tongue of the Sea of Egypt,
and will wave his hand over the River
   with his scorching breath,
and strike it into seven channels,
   and he will lead people across in sandals.
16 And there will be a highway from Assyria
   for the remnant that remains of his people,
as there was for Israel
   when they came up from the land of Egypt. (Isaiah 11.15,16)

In the prophecy of Isaiah as in the Revelation this is a figure of speech to describe the salvation work of the Messiah and not to be taken as a drying up of all the "waters". And the kings from the east are in fact those who are sent by God in the battle against evil forces. They are in fact God's faithful?
   An important teaching of the Revelation is this war between the dragon and the Christ and also between the dragon and the followers of Christ:

"**12** And the ten horns that you saw are ten kings who have not yet received royal power, but they are to receive authority as kings for one hour, together with the beast. **13** These are of one mind, and they hand over their power and authority to the beast. **14** They will make war on the Lamb, and the Lamb will conquer them, for he is Lord of lords and King of kings, and those with him are called and chosen and faithful. (17.12-14)

But is this war not continuing until the return of Christ? Is this war restricted to the battle against the forces brought together by the devil, such as the beasts and false prophet, Rome?

We know this from all the teachings given to us in all of Scripture. This is nothing new or original with the Revelation. Until the return in glory of our Lord and his angels, until the resurrection, the Church needs to stay awake and needs to remain faithful and understand how the dragon always operates. Again, this goes back to the important teachings of the apostle Paul to the Ephesians and to other churches. (Ephesians 6.10-20; Romans 16.20; 1 Thessalonians 2.18; 3.5; 2 Corinthians 2.11; 4.4; 6.15; 11.14; 12.7).

17. HOPE AND THE HOLY CITY

"**9** Then came one of the seven angels who had the seven bowls full of the seven last plagues and spoke to me, saying, "Come, I will show you the Bride, the wife of the Lamb." **10** And he carried me away in the Spirit to a great, high mountain, and showed me the holy city Jerusalem coming down out of heaven from God, **11** having the glory of God, its radiance like a most rare jewel, like a jasper, clear as crystal." (Revelation 21.9-22)

*

John, I met believers one day who were distributing Bibles in the street. They were announcing that Jesus is returning in fifty years. I asked them what difference it makes for me or anyone else if Christ is coming back in fifty years. What difference does it make if I die today and have not repented and put my trust in Jesus? After I asked this question the person did not know what to answer and was puzzled. What do you think about my reaction?

Yann, even I who spent three years with Jesus and who am an apostle, I do not know of any date we can give for the return of Jesus. Even the Revelation I received on the isle of Patmos does not give us a date.

When we were still with Jesus he told us about his coming in clouds with great power and glory and how the angels would gather his elect from the four winds, from the ends of the earth to the ends of heaven. We wanted to know about the day or hour, and he told us that no one knows, not even the angels in heaven, nor the son but only the Father. So be on guard, keep awake for you do not know when the time will come. (Mark 13.25-27). I remember also that when Jesus was with us after his resurrection and told us to stay in Jerusalem where we would receive power from heaven, we asked him the question whether this would be the time when he would restore the kingdom to Israel. But he answered us saying, "It is not for you to know times or seasons that the Father has fixed by his own authority". (Acts1.6,7). So, Yann the Revelation does not give us any day or hour and Jesus never did give us any date or hour for his return so it is not right for people to claim that in fifty years or on such a day the Lord will return.

John, how did the Christians in your time maintain their hope? What is the message of hope in the Revelation? Also, what do you think the Lord is saying to us today in an age of growing fears with things like a huge world population and the climate or whether or not the earth will continue to be a livable place in the future.

The Lord who gave us the Revelation, who himself came and walked on this earth among us, knows the human heart better than anyone else since he created this world and all of us. In

His word we are encouraged to throw away fear and embrace hope founded and rooted in him.

Today it seems difficult for many people to rest their hope on the word, the Scripture given through prophets and apostles, and on Jesus the Christ. We find many objections to our faith. I often hear that what was written so long ago or what happened so long ago cannot help us today, that we need something new, something different.

When Jesus walked on this earth and we followed him and learned from him there was strong opposition to him even when he healed the blind or resurrected the dead. He performed miracles that no one had ever performed and lived a life without any sin, but pain and suffering followed him every day of his life. Yes, when Jesus walked among us men ruled with great cruelty and practiced things that cannot even be mentioned. Remember in my Gospel that Jesus was the light who came to bring the light in the darkness.

*

When our people entered the land of Canaan, they were warned by Moses not to practice what the Canaanites were practicing, but to be different and live according to the will of the creator. The law that was given to our people was for the good of everyone. To choose the will of God was to choose life and peace. In the book *devarim* (Deuteronomy) we are taught how important making the right choice is for the happiness and well-being of our people and for all who will listen to this teaching. These are the words we find in *devarim* about this, "See, I have set before you today life and good, death and evil. If you obey the commandments of the Lord your God that I command you today, by loving the Lord your God, by walking in his ways, and by keeping his commandments and his statutes and his rules, then you shall live and multiply, and the Lord your God will bless you in the land that you are entering to take possession of it." (Deuteronomy 30.15,16).

John, today people find many objections to the Scripture, to words like these. For example, they say that those who choose the will of God and try to practice his will still face difficulties and pains. They also say that many others are not following God's will, are living contrary to his will and are still living a good life and seem blessed by God.

The Lord taught us to love our enemies. He also reminded us that the Father gives rain and sun to the righteous and the unrighteous. God continually blesses those who reject him or do not wish to listen to him.

The truth remains that viewed from God's perspective our choices will change the course of our lives as individuals or as families or nations either for good or evil. The physical circumstances of human beings do not tell the entire story about their lives. What about their souls, their eternal destiny? What about the influence they have on this earth either for good or bad?

When people object to what God has spoken through his servants the prophets or through his Son they are choosing to object, they are choosing not to believe. This is a question of trust. And if they do not trust the words revealed by God, they will need to trust their own conclusions or what someone else says. Is not this how the Scripture begins when Satan speaks and begins with the words "Did God actually say…?" (Genesis 3.1).

It is true that the entire Scripture is built on the idea that our creator has spoken and given us words to live by. It is also true that in the story of Israel we have an example of what happens when people stop trusting God and refuse to listen to his word. That is true in the Scripture but have things not changed since these Scriptures were given? Is not the population of the world much larger? Are we not facing challenges and trials that never existed before?

What you bring up here has always been the case. Those who received the law through Moses died and even their children died. At some point other generations were born and things changed for those generations. We see that in our Scriptures. Long after *devarim* (Deuteronomy) had been taught to our people we read that in the time of the judges, "everyone did what was right in his own eyes." (Judges 17.6; 21.25). Our Proverbs teach that "every way of a man is right in his own eyes, but the Lord weighs the heart." (Proverbs 21.2). The last part of *devarim* teach about the importance of choosing life, of choosing truth. But throughout the book we are taught that God's will needs to be taught by parents to children. We have received words which need to be engraved in our hearts and would help us remain faithful to God every day of our lives:

"**4** Hear, O Israel: The Lord our God, the Lord is one. You shall love the Lord your God with all your heart and with all your soul and with all your might. **5** And these words that I command you today shall be on your heart.**6** You shall teach them diligently to your children and shall talk of them when you sit in your house, and when you walk by the way, and when you lie down, and when you rise. **7** You shall bind them as a sign on your hand, and they shall be as frontlets between your eyes. **8** You shall write them on the doorposts of your house and on your gates." (Deuteronomy 6.4-9)

I remember that Jesus often reminded his listeners of the commandment you just mentioned: "You shall love the Lord your God with all your heart and with all your soul and with all your might." This commandment was given long before the time of Jesus. When Jesus spoke, everyone knew that God had spoken these words. It is difficult for me to explain this to you who walked with Jesus and grew up with the fear and respect of the Creator but in 2022 we often meet people who have no respect for God and no love for him; people who even speak with hatred about God. What would you say about this?

It is by our actions and our lives, not just our words, that we show whether we respect and love God or not. When we walked with the Lord and he taught us and our people, when he healed the sick and blessed them in so many ways his three years of work as the good shepherd were full of opposition and even hatred towards him. He even stated that if the miracles that were done in Capernaum had been done in Sodom the city would have repented. If the miracles he performed in Chorazin and Bethsaida had been done in Tyre and Sidon, they would have repented. You see Yann, we sometimes think we know people's hearts and who would listen to God or not but only God knows the heart. Remember the words of the prophet Samuel in God's choice of David as king over Israel: "For the Lord sees not as man sees, man looks on the outward appearance, but the Lord looks on the heart." (1 Samuel 16.7)

John, is this what was meant by the words of Jesus "Judge not that you be not judged"? Today, when we try and share the teachings of the Word with people, they often quote these words of Jesus to mean that nobody should point out whether they are acting unjustly or sinning. And so many of us Christians prefer to be silent when it comes to preaching or teaching the need for repentance and turning away from sin.

Certainly, the words of Jesus are an important warning about judging others. The Lord here as in many other places is giving a warning about hypocrisy. Remember the words that follow this warning about judging others,

> "**4** Or how can you say to your brother, 'Let me take the speck out of your eye,' when there is the log in your own eye? **5** You hypocrite, first take the log out of your own eye, and then you will see clearly to take the speck out of your brother's eye." (Matthew 7.4,5)

So, when we meet people who have no respect for God and even speak evil of him what should we do?

Note that Jesus taught us saying "first take the log out of your own eye". Did you notice the word "first". So here the Lord is telling us about a process, a way of doing something. We always should remember our own "log" and work on taking it out. And the log is what is making us blind, it is our own sin and failures. Jesus continued and said: "And then you will see clearly to take the speck out of your brother's eye".

Throughout his Word God is always warning us to work on ourselves, to be prayerful and loving, to be good students or disciples. He is talking about growing in our love for God and neighbor. The Lord did not tell us how each one of us will be able to take out the log from our own eye, he is just warning us to do it. He does not tell us at one point we will know how to help our brother. He is just promising us that at some point we will know what to do. This leaves each one of us with his own responsibility, his or her own need to spend time seeking the Lord and his will and being nurtured in his word. And here I return to what I said before that it is by our actions and our lives, not just our words, that we show whether we respect and love God or not.

John, are you saying that the responsibility of helping our world to be a better place to live, a better place to hope, falls first on us who claim to be the disciples of the Lord, who claim to strive to love God?

The reason for this is that it is not difficult to find fault in others or in their bad choices. When our Lord spoke, he did not say that it was really hard to see even a speck in our brother's eye. We can usually see that speck. But what is more difficult to do is to see the log in our own lives, our own hearts. So, the Lord is teaching us to focus on what is more difficult and more important. If we do that, we will be in a better position to help fellow human beings and our world.

John, what does all of this have to do with what I mentioned about our modern word? We often hear that what was written so long ago or what happened so long ago cannot help us to-day, that we need something new, something different.

The objections people bring up to you about God or the Scriptures, about Jesus or any teaching in the Scriptures should not be your main concern or the main concern of disciples liv-ing in your modern times. Yes, these objections are difficult to hear and we wish we could respond to them. You and other be-lievers would like for these people to understand things as you understand them. It is difficult to face unbelief and mistrust towards our Lord and his teachings. But as believers in your modern world face this unbelief and mistrust towards God, they must remember the words of Jesus we just mentioned. The important thing for disciples of our Lord in your modern world is for them to be able to avoid any kind of hypocrisy, is to be real, is to trust that the Lord knows best how to deal with unbe-lief. This will be as difficult for you as it was for us but just as important. You see we can easily forget our own faith in a God always at work, at our side and working on our behalf. We can easily try and do God's work in his place and forget what our work is. Remember the words of our brother and apostle Paul to the Christians in Corinth who wanted to give too much importance to some believers over others, to some teachers over others:

> "**5**What then is Apollos? What is Paul? Servants through whom you believed, as the Lord assigned to each. **6** I planted, Apollos watered, but God gave the growth. **7** So neither he who plants nor he who waters is anything, but only God who gives the growth. **8** He who plants and he who waters are one, and each will receive his wages according to his labor. **9** For we are God's fellow workers. You are God's field, God's building." (1 Corinthians 3.5-9).

John if I understand this correctly, when we face all these objections in our modern world, the main thing the Lord requires of us is to be real disciples, to be authentically trying to follow him?

Yes, and that is exactly what you and Christians in the modern world need to do. Did you notice that in the Revelation the Lord does not start by telling us all the problems in the world and the terrible behavior of the rulers in the world or even about the working of the dragon to oppose the faith? What does the Revelation begin with?

It begins with the Lord Jesus standing in the midst of the lampstands and the churches.

And why do you think it begins like this?

It begins like this because of what we have been talking about, the need for disciples of Jesus to work on their spiritual growth, on their love for God and neighbor as their priority in life.

As Christians in your modern world face all the objections of the modern world and all the arguments they bring up to reject the Gospel or teachings of our Lord, this should not distract them from what the Lord is calling them to do or how to live. Remember also that nobody can build their house on sand and be assured that the house will stand when the storm comes. Everyone has to face the need to practice the teachings of our Lord because not practicing them will have the same disastrous effects.

John, is it not true that those who choose the will of God and try to practice this will does not mean they will not face difficulties and pains?

When God spoke to our people who were going to settle in the land of the Canaanites, he gave them his commandments and made promises to them. But he did not tell them they would face no obstacle, no difficulty. He did not tell them that they would not have enemies. He did not say that death or sickness would be gone. He did not promise them an easy life without effort or without pain.

This is what is difficult for so many to understand in our modern world. If God is love and all powerful, why is there so much pain and often so many trials in life?

Well Yann, God never promised that this fallen world would one day be paradise. This you will not find in the teachings of the prophets and apostles or the teachings of Jesus our Lord. There is no such promise. Do you remember what the two greatest commands — two commands which are actually one?

Yes, they come from the law of Moses and Jesus mentioned them often:

"**37** You shall love the Lord your God with all your heart and with all your soul and with all your mind. **38** This is the great and first commandment. **39** And a second is like it: You shall love your neighbor as yourself. **40** On these two commandments depend all the Law and the Prophets." (Matthew 22.37-40)

Would you say that to keep these commands is sometimes difficult even in your modern world? Do you think it was different for us in Israel at the time of Jesus? Do you think it was different for those who lived when Jesus gave me the Revelation?

No, I don't think so. I am not sure that it was easier for you and the early disciples of Jesus to keep those commandments.
We tend to think that what we are living through is more difficult and brings more pain than what others are living through but oftentimes that is not the case. We today who saw the Lord and followed him are living in the pagan and cruel world dominated by the Empire described as one that makes war on the Lamb and the saints. (13.7; 17.14). Is the modern world you live in worse for Christians?

Today in our world we have a lot of bad things going on, people killing others and also a lot of people who have become slaves of drugs or evil practices. But I am not sure it is worse than what we read in the Revelation and what was happening to you and the first Christians.
Certainly, many of you are going through difficulties and tribulations. This is also something the Lord wants to show us in his Revelation and that is the reason the book ends with the return of the Lord and the consummation of all things.

*Here in America, there is no Roman empire that can systemati-
cally kill Christians, but we are witnessing efforts to silence
believers and punish them for their convictions. And there are
other parts of the world where Christians are being robbed of
all their belongings or put to death because of their faith.*

Yann, that is not surprising since our Lord taught us often
that there would be opposition and persecution for those who
would follow him. What you see is that the Revelation is clearly showing that even though the Lord will bring judgment on
that great persecuting power described as a terrible beast it
does not mean that life will be easy on this earth for faithful
followers of Jesus.

*Yes, John I understand this. We do have preachers today who
promise those who follow Christ that they will prosper or not
be ill as part of their walk with Christ.*

I would say that they need to read the Revelation for themselves and the entire Scriptures because pain and suffering will
be part of this earthly life for everybody until the "time for
restoring all the things about which God spoke by his holy
prophets long ago". (Acts 3.20,21). There will be pain until the
Lord returns and brings about his new heaven and new earth as
described in the Revelation.

*John, there is heaven where God resides but there is also the
promise of a new heaven and a new earth. The heaven where
God resides is eternal. But the heavens we can see as we gaze
at the stars or moon will pass away according to what the
apostle Peter wrote. Is this also what the Revelation teaches?*

In the Revelation the Lord shows his disciples that the first
heaven and the first earth will pass away and that the sea will
be no more. Also, it is at that point that the holy city, the new
Jerusalem will come down out of heaven from God, prepared

as a bride prepared by her husband. And as our brother has written, the bride of Christ is the Church, God's people (Revelation 21.1,2; Ephesians 5.22-24).

But if the heavenly city is the Church, the bride of Christ, does this mean that this "city" is mainly people rather than a place or a city such as Rome or our modern cities?

In the Revelation the Lord unveils to us his people spiritual truths about this earth and about heaven. But the heavenly realities are completely different from anything human eyes have ever seen, or human ears have ever heard. God's Word reveals such truths to us in the language we can understand which is the language of our human senses. We saw the resurrected Lord but sometimes did not immediately recognize him and he even appeared when all doors were closed. However, when he appeared to us when we were fishing, he also ate with us. (John 21.9-14).

Do you mean that the heavenly city is beyond anything we could actually describe with our human and earthly experience and in our human and earthly words?

This is the case because the coming down of the heavenly city just like the resurrection of the dead on the last day have never been part of the human experience. These realities can only be described in the language of allegory, pictures or poetry and this is the way God has revealed them to us. Remember the account of our brother Paul who was taken to paradise and how he was not able to describe "the surpassing greatness" of his revelations.

In the Revelation there is heaven and there is also a new heaven and new earth. The holy city, the new Jerusalem comes down out of heaven. At the same time the first heaven and the first earth pass away. All of this is very intriguing for the modern man.

Heaven is where we find the all-knowing God and from where God reveals himself. In the Revelation we see the throne or rule of God as directed from heaven. It is from heaven that God's plan for future generations is seen including the great opposition to Christ and his followers on the part God's adversaries, with the ancient serpent, Satan, being the main adversary and the source of all opposition and persecution. The Revelation also teaches believers of all times that their destiny and victory is safe in the hands of the Lord as he promised himself: "My sheep hear my voice, and I know them, and they follow me. I give them eternal life, and they will never perish, and no one is able to snatch them out of the Father's hand." (John 10.27,28). They are those who in the vision of the 144,000 follow the lamb and who have his name and the Father's name written on their foreheads. It is these who follow the lamb wherever he goes. (14.1-4).

All of these visions are encouraging us to maintain our hope in God's plan and promises. Before his ascension Jesus had promised to be present with his disciples until the end of the age. (Matthew 28.20). And in the Revelation, he assures us that he is coming soon: "He who testifies to these things says, 'Surely I am coming soon.' Amen. Come, Lord Jesus!" (22.20). The apostle Peter reminds us in his second epistle of scoffers coming in the last days who follow their own sinful desires and say, "Where is the promise of his coming? For ever since the fathers fell asleep, all things are continuing as they were from the beginning of creation."

Peter reminds us that with the Lord one day is as a thousand years, and a thousand years as one day.

The Lord is not slow to fulfill his promise as some count slowness, but is patient toward you, not wishing that any should perish, but that all should reach repentance. But the day of the Lord will come like a thief, and then the heavens will pass away with a roar, and the heavenly bodies will be burned up and dissolved, and the earth and the works that are done on it will be exposed.(2 Peter 3.4-10)

I noticed that you saw the holy city, the new Jerusalem coming down from heaven. This is what you saw in the vision. But this is a vision, a way for the Lord to open a window into what God has planned for his people. Is this really a description of what will happen in the future?

The Revelation is not the only time God has revealed the amazing future he has in store for the righteous. When reading of such promises we should not forget the heart of the message, the good news from God which is that we have eternal life when we "know him" and the one he sent, his son Jesus. We must remember the last words Jesus taught us during the last supper when he broke bread and shared the cup with us. These last words are his last prayer before his arrest and crucifixion. The will of the Father is for his children to be one, to love one another and to live with hearts full of joy and peace. The prayer which I recorded in my Gospel is a great lesson on how to understand God's plan for his people. (John 17).

Remember also the wonderful words given to us through Paul in his second letter to Timothy where he mentions God's purpose and grace given to us in Christ Jesus and which were manifested through His appearing; Jesus our Lord abolished death and brought to light life and immortality. (2 Timothy 1.9,10)

*

The great visions of the Revelation will not help us if they are for the most part about the physical, the material world we can perceive with our eyes and ears. Of course, this is part of God's plan, there are clear promises concerning our world and the creation. If you recall the letters to the seven churches, the Lord's will for us is in this unique love we have for Him and for one another, this unique peace and joy we have when we truly repent and trust him in all our ways. In the vision of the holy city coming down from heaven I heard a voice from the throne and the words pronounced by this voice tell us the deep meaning of this Revelation.

Remind me of these words.

The loud voice from the throne said these words, "Behold, the dwelling place of God is with man. He will dwell with them and they will be his people, and God himself will be with them as their God. He will wipe away every tear from their eyes, and death shall be no more, neither shall there be mourning, nor crying, nor pain anymore, for the former things have passed away." (Revelation 21.3,4).

Yes, John these are amazing words coming from the throne, from heaven. They tell us of wonderful promises in store for those who are faithful to God.

But there is something very important that I heard but this time from the Father, the one seated on the throne along with the lamb, "Behold, I am making all things new." (Revelation 21.5). Did you notice that now in the vision the one on the throne is speaking in the present tense when he says "I am making all things new" I want to ask you this question, when the voice says "the dwelling place of God is with man" is this about only the future?

Well, are not all of these last visions of the Revelation about the future?

Then I will ask you this question. When Jesus sent his apostles to preach the Gospel to all nations, baptizing them in the name of the Father, the Son and the Holy Spirit, did he not make a promise to them saying "Behold, I am with you always, to the end of the age." (Matthew 28.20)

Do you mean that when Jesus sends his apostles and through them all of his disciples into the world, he is already making all things new, they are already living the promise he makes in the Revelation to be with them and dwell with them?

Is this not what he taught at the last supper? Remember his words: "If anyone loves me, he will keep my word, and my Father will love him, and we will come to him and make our home with him. **24** Whoever does not love me does not keep my words. And the word that you hear is not mine but the Father's, who sent me." (John 14.23,24).

So, is the vision about the holy city and new Jerusalem about the future or not?

The vision is first of all about what exists in the presence of God, where he reigns in perfect peace, joy and love. Our Father does not change, and all good gifts come from him as wrote our brother James. In the Scriptures the bride of God describes His people. The purpose of God and his kingdom are not limited by time. We live in time, but God does not, even though he has acted and will act in human history. In his second letter to Timothy Paul writes that God's purpose was accomplished for us in Christ Jesus "before the ages began". (2 Timothy 1.9).

Is not the bride of God in the Old Testament his people, Israel?

Yes, and the Scriptures meant by that Israelites who were living faithfully in a covenant relationship with God; Israelites who were faithful to that covenant just as a wife is faithful to her husband or her husband to the wife. God is always faithful. He always tells the truth and accomplishes his promises. But he wants men and women to find him, to come to him and to live in close communion with him.

I remember the apostle Paul saying something like that when speaking in Athens, that God made from one man every nation of mankind to live on the surface of the earth; that he wanted all men to seek him and find their way toward him and find him. (Acts 17.26,27)

God's plan has always been to bless every single human being, every man and every woman throughout all nations and families of the earth. This is the calling he addressed to Abraham and Sarah that through their posterity all the families of the earth would be blessed. (Genesis 12.3; 22.18).

You said earlier that the vision is first of all about what exists in the presence of God, where he reigns in perfect peace, joy and love. Is this what the apostle Paul meant when writing to the Christians in Rome,

> *"**17** For the kingdom of God is not a matter of eating and drinking but of righteousness and peace and joy in the Holy Spirit. **18** Whoever thus serves Christ is acceptable to God and approved by men. **19** So then let us pursue what makes for peace and for mutual upbuilding." (Romans 15.17-19)*

In these words our brother Paul shows us how the kingdom of God is manifested through those who have received the wonderful gift of the Holy Spirit. The kingdom of God is to be lived out and expressed in the world by followers of Jesus who live at peace with one another, who live in righteousness and who are full of joy.

Is this also what the apostle teaches to the Christians in Galatia concerning the fruit of the Holy Spirit?

Yes, and he mentions clearly what this fruit of the Spirit consists of in the life of a disciple: love, joy, peace, patience, kindness, goodness, faithfulness, gentleness and self-control. (Galatians 5.22,23). He even teaches that those who do evil things which he describes as "works of the flesh" such as sexual immorality or jealousy will not inherit the kingdom of God. (Galatians 5.19,21)

John, how is all of this connected to the vision of the holy city, the new Jerusalem coming down from heaven?

Well Yann you just answered your question.

How is that?

The answer is in the description of the city as being holy. It is also in the description of the bride adorned for her husband. In the letter he wrote to our brethren in Ephesus the apostle Paul described the Church as being the bride of Christ. He taught us about how this marriage was made possible:

> "**25** Husbands, love your wives, as Christ loved the church and gave himself up for her, **26** that he might sanctify her, having cleansed her by the washing of water with the word, **27** so that he might present the church to himself in splendor, without spot or wrinkle or any such thing, that she might be holy and without blemish." (Ephesians 5.25-27).

I have a question concerning this teaching of the apostle Paul concerning the bride of Christ. How can the Church be the bride of Christ (thus of God) while Israel is also the bride of God? Has one bride replaced another?

No Yann, the Word of God is not describing for us two brides of God. Why would you think that the bride of Christ (or God) in Ephesians is different from the bride of God as Israel?

When he uses the word "church" is Paul not alluding to the Gentiles, to non-Jews?

That is not the case because in the same letter to the Christians in Ephesus the apostle Paul makes it clear that he is first of all writing about Israel. The explanation of Paul is very clear. Through him the Holy Spirit teaches us that "gentiles were at one time separated from Christ, alienated from the commonwealth of Israel and strangers to the covenants of promise, having no hope and without God in the world." He continues by writing that "So then now you are no longer strangers and aliens, but you are fellow citizens with the saints and members of the household of God…" (See Ephesians 2.11-22). Were not the first three thousand baptized on Pentecost from Israel? (Acts chapter 2).

Gentiles in Christ are not a separate body of believers from Israel, they are "fellow heirs, members of the same body and partakers of the promise in Christ Jesus through the Gospel". (Ephesians 3.6). In his letter to the Christians in Galatia the apostle teaches the same truth, writing that "For as many of you as were baptized into Christ have put on Christ. There is neither Jew nor Greek, there is neither slave nor free, there is no male and female, for you are all one in Christ Jesus. And if you are Christ's, then you are Abraham's offspring, heirs according to promise." (Galatians 3.28,29).

The new Jerusalem you saw coming down from heaven is "holy", is a bride prepared for her husband. So, it is not a city made of stones and buildings?

This is also what is meant by not adding to the Revelation or taking away from it. We add and take away whenever we use the Revelation as a teaching or a vision that is not in harmony with the teachings of Christ and his apostles. Those who read this prophecy are blessed if they keep what is written in it. (Revelation 22.18,19; 1.3).

*

12 I must go on boasting. Though there is nothing to be gained by it, I will go on to visions and revelations of the Lord. **2** I know a man in Christ who fourteen years ago was caught up to the third heaven—whether in the body or out of the body I do not know, God knows. **3** And I know that this man was caught up into paradise—whether in the body or out of the body I do not know, God knows— **4** and he heard things that cannot be told, which man may not utter. **5** On behalf of this man I will boast, but on my own behalf I will not boast, except of my weaknesses— **6** though if I should wish to boast, I would not be a fool, for I would be speaking the truth; but I refrain from it, so that no one may think more of me than he sees in me or hears from me. **7** So to keep me from becoming conceited because of the surpassing greatness of the revelations, a thorn was given me in the flesh, a messenger of Satan to harass me, to keep me from becoming conceited. (2 Corinthians 12.1-7)

9 Then came one of the seven angels who had the seven bowls full of the seven last plagues and spoke to me, saying, "Come, I will show you the Bride, the wife of the Lamb." **10** And he carried me away in the Spirit to a great, high mountain, and showed me the holy city Jerusalem coming down out of heaven from God, **11** having the glory of God, its radiance like a most rare jewel, like a jasper, clear as crystal. **12** It had a great, high wall, with twelve gates, and at the gates twelve angels, and on the gates the names of the twelve tribes of the sons of Israel were inscribed — **13** on the east three gates, on the north three gates, on the south three gates, and on the west three gates. **14** And the wall of the city had twelve foundations, and on them were the twelve names of the twelve apostles of the Lamb. (Revelation 21.9-14)

18. THE NEW HEAVENS AND NEW EARTH

21 Then I saw a new heaven and a new earth, for the first heaven and the first earth had passed away, and the sea was no more. **2** And I saw the holy city, new Jerusalem, coming down out of heaven from God, prepared as a bride adorned for her husband. (Revelation 21.1,2)

*

How then are we to understand the new heavens and new earth if the holy city is not a material and physical city?

What we need to understand is that the fact that it is not essentially material and physical in the way we now see and touch does not mean it is not real. God is real and we do not see him; he is "spirit" as our Lord taught the woman of Samaria. The woman asked where God should be worshipped – in Jerusalem or on mount Gerizim in Samaria – and the Lord taught her neither: God must be worshipped from a pure and sincere heart, in truth and in spirit.

Is this to be understood the same way as the statement about God's presence among his people, "He will dwell with them, and they will be his people" (Rev. 21.3)

This is also the truth preached by the deacon Stephen before his stoning when he also quoted the prophet Amos: "The Most High does not dwell in houses made by hands". (Acts 7.48).

Did not the prophet Isaiah also prophesy about a new heaven and new earth? And did not the apostle Peter also prophesy about the destruction of the earth and how we are waiting for new heavens and a new earth in which righteousness dwells?

The words of the Revelation concerning the new heavens and new earth are confirmed and taught elsewhere in the inspired Scriptures, especially in the letters of Peter and the prophecy of Isaiah. (2 Peter 3.1-18; Isaiah 65.17-25). These prophecies and teachings are about God's intervention in favor of his people under opposition and even persecution from unbelieving and sinful people. Our brother Peter teaches this in both of his letters. At the same time, he exhorts these Christians not to be ashamed of the name Christian but on the contrary to live up to God's calling to be holy. Isaiah the prophet speaks under divine inspiration to those who have been taken as exiles away from their land and have remained faithful. The prophecy is also a warning to those who do not listen and do not consider the work of the Lord's servant. (Isaiah 65.8-16). The new heavens and new earth describe how the "former troubles are forgotten", how "the former things shall not be remembered or come into mind", how these former pains will be replaced by rejoicing and gladness. This is the same lesson to our brethren in the Revelation when God wipes away all tears from their eyes. (Rev. 21.4). The apostle Peter teaches that the new earth God will create is one where righteousness dwells.

So, are we to expect at some future point the creation by God of new heavens and a new earth?

The God who created the world in six days is an all-powerful God. His creation is a work of his supernatural power and this power and knowledge of God is beyond our comprehension. It is by this power that the Lord Jesus changed the water into wine, healed the blind man and raised Lazarus from the dead. Our brother Paul writes to the church in Ephesus that we are called to know "the love of Christ that surpasses knowledge", that the Lord "is able to far more abundantly than all we ask or think, according to the power at work within us." (Ephesians 3.18-21). Yes, we are to expect great things from our God and things that are beyond what our earthly language is able to describe. This was also the witness of Paul who was taken up to the third heaven, not knowing whether or not he was in his body, and where he heard things that cannot be told, which man may not utter. (2 Corinthians 12.1-4).

John, science has made great progress in 2022 and most people do not believe God created all things in six days or that he will bring about new heavens and a new earth. It is difficult to talk today about such topics.

Yes, I understand that. But it is also very difficult for brethren living in the Roman empire to talk about these things. The Greeks and Romans have their own understanding of how the earth was created or how it will end. Man does not always understand or accept the thinking of God. In the prophet Isaiah the Lord God speaks calling people to seek him and forsake wickedness — also saying

"**8** For my thoughts are not your thoughts, neither are
your ways my ways, declares the Lord. **9** For as the
heavens are higher than the earth, so are my ways
higher than your ways and my thoughts than your
thoughts." (Isaiah 55.8,9).

Your modern science cannot explain a universe created in six
days just as it cannot explain a man coming back from the dead
or water changed into wine. There is a reason why the Scriptures calls these things miracles or signs. We can talk about the
"miracle" of creation; even the "miracle" of the creation of a
baby in the mother's womb as Psalm 139 testifies. And we
could also talk about the miracle of the new creation through
the power of the Gospel, the new birth in Spirit and water. Our
brother Paul writes about conversion and coming to Christ as a
"new creation" because it is only made possible by God's direct intervention. And we could add to this the resurrection of
the dead promised by our Lord Jesus and the teachings of his
apostles.

There were Christians in Corinth who were asking the following questions concerning the resurrection: "How are the dead
raised? With what kind of body do they come?" (1 Corinthians
15.35). Paul under divine inspiration gives answers to such
questions and also writes that "If there is a natural body; there
is also a spiritual body". Talking about Adam who came from
the dust or earth and the saints who are raised from the dead,
the apostle says,

"**47** The first man was from the earth, a man of
dust; the second man is from heaven. **48** As was the
man of dust, so also are those who are of the dust, and
as is the man of heaven, so also are those who are of
heaven. **49** Just as we have borne the image of the man

of dust, we shall also bear the image of the man of heaven." (1 Corinthians 15.47-49)

So, there will be new heavens and a new earth just as there will be a resurrection from the dead. Can we say that, as yet we know very little about what that means? That this promise remains clouded in our understanding?

Just as we do not know what we will be when the Lord appears as I wrote in one of my letters:

"**1** See what kind of love the Father has given to us, that we should be called children of God; and so, we are. The reason why the world does not know us is that it did not know him. **2** Beloved, we are God's children now, and what we will be has not yet appeared; but we know that when he appears, we shall be like him, because we shall see him as he is. **3** And everyone who thus hopes in him purifies himself as he is pure." (1 John 3.1-3)

God's promises are given to us as foundations to build our hope on. The writer to the Hebrews reminds us that faith is not about what we can see but about what we hope for and we cannot see. (Hebrews 11.1). The apostle Paul also teaches this in his letter to the Romans concerning the creation which will be set free from its bondage to corruption at the revealing of the children of God, their resurrection. (Romans 8.18-25). What we hope for is not seen, it is still a promise from God,

"**23** And not only the creation, but we ourselves, who have the firstfruits of the Spirit, groan inwardly as we wait eagerly for adoption as sons, the redemption of our bodies. **24** For in this hope we were saved. Now hope that is seen is not hope. For who hopes for

what he sees? **25** But if we hope for what we do not
see, we wait for it with patience." (Romans 8.23-25).

*

Ralph Erskine (1685-1752)

A new-made world appear'd so gay,
The old was no more seen;
Heav'n, earth, and sea were roll'd away,
As if they ne'er had been.

Jerus'lem new came from above,
Like Paradise restor'd,
Prepar'd, as when the bride of love
Is deck'd to meet her Lord.

The shouting Heav'ns cry'd out, Behold,
God's dwelling is with man!
They shall be his; he'll keep his hold,
And be their God and gain.

His tender hand shall wipe the tears
From ev'ry weeping eye;
And pains, and groans, and griefs, and fears,
And death itself, shall die.

The former things away are fled,
To be no more in view:
He sat upon the throne, who said,
Lo! I make all things new.

I'm Alpha and Omega too,
The origin and end:
Unto my royal orders now,
Let mortals all attend:

To him that thirsts, I'll freely give,
O' th' well of life his fill;
And he that drinks shall ever live,
Come whosoever will.

The saint that conquers sin, shall be
Of all things heir by line;
For I shall be his God, and he
A son and heir of mine.

But whoremongers, adulterers,
Despising God's commands,
Idolaters and sorcerers,
And men of bloody hands;

The faithless, and the scoffing crew,
That spurn at offer'd grace:
The devil's sordid retinue,
And all the lying race:

These shall be doom'd all to partake
Of ever-burning wrath;
And thrown into the fiery lake,
Which is the second death.

But happy on the other side,
Appear the heirs of life:

Heav'n's glory crowns the beauteous bride,
The Lamb's beloved wife.[1]

---

[1] Ralph Erskine, *The Revelation - Song 13: The New Heaven and New Earth.*

19. HOLINESS

"**10** And he said to me, 'Do not seal up the words of the prophecy of this book, for the time is near. **11** Let the evildoer still do evil, and the filthy still be filthy, and the righteous still do right, and the holy still be holy.' **12** 'Behold, I am coming soon, bringing my recompense with me, to repay each one for what he has done. **13** I am the Alpha and the Omega, the first and the last, the beginning and the end.'" Revelation 22.10-13)

*

It is surprising that the Lord says not to seal the words of the prophecy of this book, for the time is near.

Yann, consider the words of God to the prophet Daniel who was told the opposite::

"**8** Then I said, 'O my lord, what shall be the outcome of these things?' **9** He said, "Go your way, Daniel, for the words are shut up and sealed until the time of the end. **10** Many shall purify themselves and make themselves white and be refined, but the wicked shall act wickedly. And none of the wicked shall understand, but those who are wise shall understand. (Daniel 12.8-10)

Daniel was then living under the rule of the Persian kings, so that was long before the events he prophesied about the coming Messiah and future events that would occur.

Exactly. And so, we can understand in the Revelation that there is a coming judgment on the persecuting forces at work against the saints during the early years of the Church as we are witnesses today. But this does not mean that the warnings given to unrepentant and evil people and rulers are not valid for all times and all places. We do not need for God to give us a timetable of all events throughout human history to understand his judgments and his calling to repentance and holy living. The God who judged the beasts of the Revelation and the prostitute is also the God who will judge the great dragon and that judgment happens at the glorious return of our Lord Jesus. The judgment of God's enemies is God's prerogative and depends on his timing. This is not for us to know when it will happen for no one knows the day and hour of the Lord's return, as mentioned by our brother the apostle Paul in some of his letters. (1 Thessalonians 5.1-11)

John, does the Lord really want people to continue to do evil and live unrighteous lives? Can you explain to me the meaning of these words at the end of the Revelation?

Yann, this comes at the end of the Revelation and especially following the glorious pictures of the Lord's return and the coming down of the heavenly Jerusalem. The Revelation has described to us the warnings and judgments of God on rebellious people who are determined to do evil and to hurt God's people. Going back to the story of the Exodus from Egypt, the Revelation has depicted to us the consequences of people hardening their hearts through sin. God's trumpets and even plagues are meant to bring people to humility and obedience, to repentance and holiness of life. Death and destruction are often the result of the evil that is sown in the human heart and the sin of hurting and murdering others.

The beast and its heads have crushed populations and have uttered blasphemies against God and his Messiah. All of this is not without consequences. It should never be forgotten that the Lord "repays each one" for what he has done unless they come back to him, unless they trust him and obey. Remember the words that accompany the blowing of the sixth trumpet:

> "**20** The rest of mankind, who were not killed by these plagues, did not repent of the works of their hands nor give up worshiping demons and idols of gold and silver and bronze and stone and wood, which cannot see or hear or walk, **21** nor did they repent of their murders or their sorceries or their sexual immorality or their thefts." (9.20,21)

Was this not what the Lord was telling the churches in Asia at the beginning of the Revelation?

The warnings to flee evil behavior and sinfulness are first given to the churches in Asia. So, in the Revelation, and in fact in all of the Scriptures, this is not a message reserved for unbelievers or those who persecute God's people. It reminds us of the words of our brother Peter in his first letter:

> "**12**Beloved, do not be surprised at the fiery trial when it comes upon you to test you, as though something

strange were happening to you. **13** But rejoice insofar as you share Christ's sufferings, that you may also rejoice and be glad when his glory is revealed. **14** If you are insulted for the name of Christ, you are blessed, because the Spirit of glory and of God rests upon you. **15** But let none of you suffer as a murderer or a thief or an evildoer or as a meddler. **16** Yet if anyone suffers as a Christian, let him not be ashamed, but let him glorify God in that name. **17** For it is time for judgment to begin at the household of God; and if it begins with us, what will be the outcome for those who do not obey the gospel of God? **18** And 'If the righteous is scarcely saved, what will become of the ungodly and the sinner?' **19** Therefore let those who suffer according to God's will entrust their souls to a faithful Creator while doing good." (1 Peter 4.12-19)

*How should we understand the words of the Lord when he says, "**14** Blessed are those who wash their robes, so that they may have the right to the tree of life and that they may enter the city by the gates." (22.14)*

These words from our Lord Jesus remind us of the sermon he preached on the mount, announcing God's blessings on those who would listen to him and practice his teachings. (Matthew 5.1-11). They also remind us of the very first Psalm declaring blessings on those who are faithful to God's law and are like trees planted by waters and which bring good fruit.

How can someone even today be washed from their sins and evil ways?

The Lord Jesus came and died for that reason, to make this possible. It is a matter of grace, not of human efforts. In order to be washed from one's sins, to receive God's forgiveness, human beings are called to believe in the Lord who died for them. They also need to repent. Remember the words of the sixth trumpet, "The rest of mankind, who were not killed by these plagues, did not repent of the works of their hands..." (9.20). Remember also the words of the Lord to the Church in Laodicea:

> "**19** Those whom I love, I reprove and discipline, so be zealous and repent. **20** Behold, I stand at the door and knock. If anyone hears my voice and opens the door, I will come in to him and eat with him, and he with me. **21** The one who conquers, I will grant him to sit with me on my throne, as I also conquered and sat down with my Father on his throne. **22** He who has an ear, let him hear what the Spirit says to the churches.' (3.19-21)

John the Baptist and even Jesus preached repentance.
The Lord called people to repent from the start of his ministry. As the people were presented with the right and loving behavior willed by God, they needed to choose this behavior and abandon their sinful ways. This has always been the case as for example when God spoke to the people of Israel before they entered the promised land,

> "**19** I call heaven and earth to witness against you today, that I have set before you life and death, blessing and curse. Therefore, choose life, that you and your offspring may live, **20** loving the Lord your God, obeying his voice and holding fast to him, for he is your life and length of days, that you may dwell in the land that the Lord swore to your fathers, to Abraham, to Isaac, and to Jacob, to give them." (Deuteronomy 30.19,20)

A good way to understand what the Lord means by "repentance" would be to look back at the warning given to the Churches in Asia.

These warning are important and are given at the beginning of the Revelation so that Christians will first of all consider their ways.

But the sins mentioned in the case of the Churches in Asia or even elsewhere in the Bible, are they still "sins" even for us today?

Why do you think the Lord brought into his Revelation pictures of how all things will end, how the Lord will bring judgment as well as blessings? Don't you think that God is this way to warning all generations of believers and all peoples until the end? Did not the Lord Jesus teach us about the great day of judgment as he spoke also about the coming destruction of the temple? (Matthew 24, 25)

I noticed that not all the churches in the Revelation are called by God to repent.

The churches in Smyrna and Philadelphia only receive praise from the Lord and are not called to repentance like the other five churches. (2.8-11; 3.712).

What was unique about these churches?

The church in Smyrna is poor and threatened by those who are at war with Christ and His Gospel. These brethren are told that some will be thrown in prison, that they will go through tribulation. The church in Philadelphia has only little power and has kept God's word with patient endurance. These brethren are also told that an hour of trial is coming upon the entire world. These warnings of coming trials are constant in the Revelation as we have seen before. The beast which persecuted Christians is about to return and hurt them even more.

Remember the teachings of James concerning those who are rich and powerful as opposed to those who are poor and vulnerable in this world:

> "**5** Listen, my beloved brothers, has not God chosen those who are poor in the world to be rich in faith and heirs of the kingdom, which he has promised to those who love him? **6** But you have dishonored the poor man. Are not the rich the ones who oppress you, and the ones who drag you into court? **7** Are they not the ones who blaspheme the honorable name by which you were called?" (James 2.5-7)

Holiness is to be pursued always, on a daily basis.
The holiness of God is emphasized in the Revelation especially in the vision of the throne and the four living creatures:

> "Holy, holy, holy, is the Lord God Almighty,
>   who was and is and is to come!" (Revelation 4.8b)

> **11** "Worthy are you, our Lord and God,
>   to receive glory and honor and power,
> for you created all things,
>   and by your will they existed and were created.
> (Revelation 4.11).

This vision is important and helps us understand how God is calling his people to holiness as he is holy, to a life without evil and sinfulness as he is without evil and sinfulness. Our brother Peter reminds us of this in his first letter:

> "**13** Therefore, preparing your minds for
> action, and being sober-minded, set your hope fully on
> the grace that will be brought to you at the revelation

of Jesus Christ. **14** As obedient children, do not be conformed to the passions of your former ignorance, **15** but as he who called you is holy, you also be holy in all your conduct, **16** since it is written, 'You shall be holy, for I am holy.'" (1 Peter 1.13-16).

The apostle Paul also describes the Church as a holy people (Ephesians 5.1-4). Those who have been washed of their sins by the sacrifice of our Lord must use their bodies as a living sacrifice, holy and pleasing to God. (Romans 12.1)

*

"How long shall we love riches? For I shall not cease exclaiming against them: for they are the cause of everything. How long do we not get our fill of this insatiable desire? What is the good of gold? I am astonished at the thing! There is some enchantment in the business, that gold and silver should be so highly valued among us. For our own souls indeed we have no regard, but those lifeless images engross much attention. Whence is it that this disease has invaded the world? Who shall be able to effect its destruction? What reason can cut off this evil beast, and destroy it with utter destruction?"[1]

---

[1] John Chrysostom 347-407 A.D, *Tenth Homily on I Thessalonians.*

20. THE MARRIAGE OF THE LAMB

6 Then I heard what seemed to be the voice of a great multitude, like the roar of many waters and like the sound of mighty peals of thunder, crying out, "Hallelujah!
For the Lord our God
   the Almighty reigns.
7 Let us rejoice and exult
   and give him the glory,
for the marriage of the Lamb has come,
   and his Bride has made herself ready;
8 it was granted her to clothe herself
   with fine linen, bright and pure"—
for the fine linen is the righteous deeds of the saints.
(Revelation 19.6-8)

Towards the end the Revelation describes the great vision of the "marriage of the lamb". I thought the Church is already married to the lamb. How can we understand this? What is this marriage of the lamb described in the Revelation?

The marriage of the lamb in the Revelation is not anything new or surprising. The Lord is not teaching us about this beautiful relationship between him and his Church as if before this vision the Church is not married to Christ or as if we needed to wait until the return of the Lord for this marriage to happen.

This is the way so many people today understand this vision.

The beautiful visions of the glorious Lord and his wonderful relationship to the Church need to be understood in light of the teachings already given to us by our Lord and his apostles, such as the letters of Paul or Peter to disciples and churches. It is clear from these writings that the Church is already living this beautiful relationship the Scriptures call "marriage".

In my Gospel the Lord's Spirit inspired me to describe Jesus' first sign of his ministry which was the changing of water into wine during the wedding at Cana. Remember also that afterwards I recorded the words of John the Baptist when a discussion arose between his disciples and the disciples of Jesus over the fact that greater numbers were being baptized at the preaching of Jesus:

> "**28** You yourselves bear me witness, that I said, 'I am not the Christ, but I have been sent before him.' **29** The one who has the bride is the bridegroom. The friend of the bridegroom, who stands and hears him, rejoices greatly at the bridegroom's voice. Therefore, this joy of mine is now complete. **30** He must increase, but I must decrease.'" (John 3.28,30)

The Baptist here was teaching about the importance of the "bridegroom" who is the Christ over the bridegroom's friend who stands and hears him, who is a helper and witness at the wedding of the bridegroom. The bridegroom's friend was John the Baptist who came to prepare the way for the Christ. Our Scriptures often described God's relationship to his people as that of a bride to a bridegroom, of a wife to a husband. Thus, the Gospel here already teaches us about the beautiful relationship of the Christ to his Church, to all his followers, his disciples.

Is this description of the Messiah's salvation work as a marriage also found in the Scriptures given to Israel?
This is the case for example in Psalm 45 which is a song about the wedding of a king. This is about the wedding of the "anointed one", the Messiah (v.7). It is also a wedding that embraces "all peoples" (v. 18). This Psalm is also very important since it is quoted (v. 8) in the letter to the Hebrews written to Christians:

> **8** "But of the Son he says, 'Your throne, O God, is forever and ever, the scepter of uprightness is the scepter of your kingdom. **9** You have loved righteousness and hated wickedness; therefore God, your God, has anointed you with the oil of gladness beyond your companions.'" (Hebrews 1.8,9).

Remember also that the prophets described the Messiah as the bridegroom: "I will rejoice greatly in the Lord, my soul will exult in my God; for He has clothed me with garments of salvation, he has wrapped me with a robe of righteousness, as a bridegroom decks himself with a garland, and as a bride adorns herself with her jewels." (Isaiah 61.10)

The kingdom of heaven is also compared by our Lord to ten virgins who took their lamps and went out to meet the bridegroom. (Matthew 25.1-12). But could we understand this as the actual marriage of the Church and the lamb while the other teachings in Scripture are more about the engagement that precedes the marriage?

Yann, this not how the writings of the apostles describe the relationship of Christ and the Church. Our brethren have already suffered and are about to suffer the greatest persecutions. Many will be put to death and will lose their loved ones in death. How would they be encouraged by a vision that is about some future event? Why would this vision not be a confirmation of the relationship of Christ and the Church which already exists and will exist for eternity and cannot be broken, even by the most difficult and terrifying events?

I believe we today read the Revelation as a vision of the future, especially as a vision of what happens at the return of our Lord Jesus in glory.

Of course, this applies to the future because what is true today about Christ and the Church cannot be untrue tomorrow or in hundreds of years in the future. We also need to understand the difference between what is not seen of the heavenly realities and what is seen.

What do you mean by that?

The relationship of Christ and the Church is one of marriage and a beautiful life of love, peace and joy. God and his people will not be reconciled, they are already reconciled. The Lord already stands in the midst of the lampstands which beyond the churches in Asia describe the local congregations or churches spread throughout the world. There is already a relationship between Christ and his disciples that is well described by the love within the couple, within marriage. Our brother Paul wrote to the church in Ephesus, saying:

> "**3** Blessed be the God and Father of our Lord Jesus Christ, who has blessed us in Christ with every spiritual blessing in the heavenly places, **4** even as he chose us in him before the foundation of the world, that we should be holy and blameless before him." (Ephesians 1.3,4)

This clearly means that the apostle Paul writing to the saints in Ephesus considers them as already blessed in Christ with every spiritual blessing.

This is the case despite the fact that these brethren as all of our brethren until the Lord's return go through pains and suffering. These pains do not separate us from the love of God, as taught by brother Paul in his letter to the Romans. (Romans 8.31-39). But note how these blessings of those who are in Christ existed even before the foundation of the world. The apostle will repeat this idea of God's "predestination" of his people even at the beginning of this letter:

> "**5** he predestined us for adoption to himself as sons through Jesus Christ, according to the purpose of his will, **6** to the praise of his glorious grace, with which he has blessed us in the Beloved." (Ephesians 1.5).

> "**11** In him we have obtained an inheritance, having been predestined according to the purpose of him who works all things according to the counsel of his will, **12** so that we who were the first to hope in Christ might be to the praise of his glory." (Ephesians 1.11).

How could we believe in God's fairness and justice if those who are saved have already been chosen and predestined from all eternity? This is very difficult to understand.

But think about this: would it not be astonishing that God would be surprised by everything that is happening or will happen? Do we not see throughout the Scriptures how God is able to reveal events of the future, something that men are unable to do? God being who he is, eternal and omniscient, would it not be contrary to his nature to ignore anything about the past, present and future? What the apostle Paul is telling the brethren in Ephesus is that all their blessings, their salvation and future hope are in the hands of a gracious and powerful God; that these brethren are not blessed in Christ by anything they can boast about. This is confirmed throughout the entire letter to these brethren.

Note also that the choosing of the saints by God is not an arbitrary choosing on the part of God. The apostle says that God "chose us in Christ". It is Christ and his work that explain this choosing not simply an arbitrary decision on the part of God for some to be saved and others not to be saved. The will of God is that "in Christ" there would be blessings in the heavenly places for the "faithful", for the "saints". Our brother Peter wrote saying that God wants all men to repent and be saved:

> "**8** But do not overlook this one fact, beloved, that with the Lord one day is as a thousand years, and a thousand years as one day. **9** The Lord is not slow to fulfill his promise as some count slowness, but is patient toward you, not wishing that any should perish, but that all should reach repentance." (2 Peter 3.8,9)

I want to go back to the difference you mentioned between the unseen and the seen. What do you mean by that?

When we look again at this letter of brother Paul to the brethren in Ephesus, we learn that they are "blessed in Christ with every spiritual blessing in the heavenly places". (Ephesians 1.3)

But do we see the "heavenly places"? Do we experience the heavenly places as long as we are on this earth? So, this teaching of the apostle Paul is also about a promise. What the saints already enjoy is what they will enjoy for eternity. Paul also wrote to the brethren in Rome concerning God's promises for the future saying:

"**22** For we know that the whole creation has been groaning together in the pains of childbirth until now. **23** And not only the creation, but we ourselves, who have the firstfruits of the Spirit, groan inwardly as we wait eagerly for adoption as sons, the redemption of our bodies. **24** For in this hope we were saved. Now hope that is seen is not hope. For who hopes for what he sees? **25** But if we hope for what we do not see, we wait for it with patience." (Romans 8.22-25)

How can the blessings already enjoyed be also for the future? How can they already be real and also be part of the hope we have?

The apostle explains it by saying that "we ourselves have the firstfruits of the Spirit". The promises of God for the future are not only promises. With these promises the saints have received the "firstfuits" of what they will receive which is the wonderful gift of the Holy Spirit. It is also to the brethren in Ephesus that the apostle Paul wrote about the saints, saying:

"**13** In him you also, when you heard the word of truth, the gospel of your salvation, and believed in him, were sealed with the promised Holy Spirit, **14** who is the

guarantee of our inheritance until we acquire possession of it, to the praise of his glory." (Ephesians
1.13,14).

*I remember how in the Revelation we see the saints having
been sealed by God with his name. Is this the same truth?*

The saints in Revelation are sealed by God, they are set apart
this way as belonging to him and under his protection (Revelation 7.2,3; 14.1,2). The Holy Spirit is God as well as the Son.
They are three and one as taught in our Scriptures. The Spirit
given to Jesus' followers is also the Spirit of Christ and he is
the Spirit of our Father (Romans 8.9-11; 2 Corinthians
3.17,18). Those who come to faith in the Lord and repent of
their sins are to be immersed "in the name of the Father, the
Son and the Holy Spirit" according to our Lord's command to
evangelize the world (Matthew 28.18,19). The one who conquers will be a "pillar in the temple of my God" and the Lord
says: "I will write on him the name of my God" (Revelation
3.12,13).

*For people living today what is unseen is often thought of as
not being real, not existing. They do not see God thus do not
believe in Him.*

When the Scripture teaches us about the not seen or unseen
this does not means that everything related to our faith has
been unseen or is unseen. The Lord Jesus was really seen by us
even after his resurrection. We preached the good news of salvation as witnesses of what we have heard, touched and seen,
as I wrote in my first letter.

*I remember that. And in this same letter you also wrote these
words:*

"3 See what kind of love the Father has given to us, that we should be called children of God, and so we are. The reason why the world does not know us is that it did not know him. 2 Beloved, we are God's children now, and what we will be has not yet appeared; but we know that when he appears, we shall be like him, because we shall see him as he is. 3 And everyone who thus hopes in him purifies himself as he is pure." (1 John 3.1-3).

So, the marriage wedding of the lamb and the Church is both about the present and the future. We can even say that it is about the past. It is the same truth as taught by Paul to the Ephesians concerning the spiritual blessings enjoyed by the saints in the heavenly places. (Ephesians 1.3,4). God is not to be understood as living within the confines of time, of past, present or future. He is the eternal one as the Revelation reminds us so often, repeating for us the words of the prophet Isaiah: "Thus says the Lord, the King of Israel and his Redeemer, the Lord of hosts: 'I am the first and I am the last, and there is no God besides Me." (Isaiah 44.6). "Listen to Me, O Jacob, even Israel whom I called; I am He, I am the first, I am also the last." (Isaiah 48.12). The Revelation quotes this truth and applies to our heavenly Father as well as to our Lord Jesus (1.8; 1.17,18; 2.8; 21.6,7; 22.13).

"I am the Alpha and the Omega," says the Lord God, "who is and who was and who is to come, the Almighty." (Revelation 1.8)

"And to the angel of the church in Smyrna write: 'The words of the first and the last, who died and came to life." (Revelation 2.8)

"17 When I saw him, I fell at his feet as though dead. But he laid his right hand on me, saying, "Fear not, I am the first and the last, **18** and the living one. I died, and behold I am alive forevermore, and I have the keys of Death and Hades." (Revelation 1.17,18).

*

"Ignatius, also called Theophorus, to the Church at Ephesus in Asia . . . predestined from eternity for a glory that is lasting and unchanging, united and chosen through true suffering by the will of the Father in Jesus Christ our God"[1]

---

[1] Ignatius of Antioch, *Letter to the Ephesians 1* [A.D. 110].

21. THE WATER OF LIFE

"On the last and greatest day of the festival, Jesus stood and said in a loud voice, "Let anyone who is thirsty come to me and drink." (John 7.37)

"**6** And he said to me, 'These words are trustworthy and true. And the Lord, the God of the spirits of the prophets, has sent his angel to show his servants what must soon take place.'"**7** "And behold, I am coming soon. Blessed is the one who keeps the words of the prophecy of this book." (Revelation 22.6,7)

16 "I, Jesus, have sent my angel to testify to you about these things for the churches. I am the root and the descendant of David, the bright morning star." **17** The Spirit and the Bride say, "Come." And let the one who hears say, "Come." And let the one who is thirsty come; let the one who desires take the water of life without price. (Revelation 22.16,17)

*

The Lord said three times at the end of the Revelation "Behold, I am coming soon." (22.7,12,20). Is this the promise of his return for the judgment and for the resurrection? For us who live over two thousand years after his ascension, will his return be soon? Can we know the time of his return and preach it?

Yann, the Lord is speaking here as in the beginning of the Revelation to us who are now going through a terrible persecution from the beast, the prostitute and the false prophet at the instigation of the great dragon. Remember how the dragon tried to drown the woman, God's people, how it became furious and declared war on the rest of her offspring, on those who keep the commandments of God and hold to the testimony of Jesus. (12.15-17; 1.9).

Remember the fifth seal. Remember the words of our martyrs under the altar, slain for their faith, for the word of God and the witness they had borne – crying to God with a loud voice, "O Sovereign Lord, holy and true, how long before you will judge and avenge our blood on those who dwell on the earth?" (6.9,10).

Yes, I do remember but here the Lord is promising that he is coming soon. And now we who are living over two thousand years later we are still waiting for his return. Can we now expect his return?

Who are the ones asking for God's judgment and justice in the fifth seal? Are they not those mentioned from the beginning and throughout the Revelation who are now under threat of death and destruction through the workings of the beasts and the great prostitute? Is the Revelation not speaking to them when the vision says,

"**11** Then they were each given a white robe and told to rest a little longer, until the number of their fellow servants and their brothers should be complete, who were to be killed as they themselves had been." (6.11)

But should we not teach about the return of the Lord in glory, his judgment and the resurrection of the dead?

Yes, we should teach these truths. But as you preach or teach in your future world can you say to those who hear you that "the Lord is coming soon" when talking about his final return? Did not the apostles teach us in their letters that the Lord will return as a thief in the night, that we are not in fact to teach people as if we knew the time or period of his return?

Yes, that seems very important and I would like to look more into this. But in this case why does the Lord talk about his "coming" if it is not about the glorious day of the resurrection and the final judgment?

Oftentimes in our Scriptures when the Lord judges a people or sinners it is described as a "coming of the Lord" so that we will understand that God himself is behind these events. Note how in the beginning of the Revelation God is described as the one "who is and who was and who is to come". (1.4). There is no absence of God from any part of human history or the history of his people. God is not the God of the dead but the living. He is the God of Abraham, Isaac and Jacob. He is the unchanging God "with whom there is no variation or shadow due to change" (James 1.17).

God has come before, he is coming now, and he will be coming in the future. The lessons of the Scriptures and the truths of the Revelation are true today and will be true tomorrow. The comfort we are being given today through the Revelation is for all of us who are to be put to death by the beast. These are lessons for all faithful disciples who will live until the Lord returns in glory.

I understand how the lessons of the Revelation are for us today and will be for disciples in the future as long as the world continues.

Myself here in Patmos and my brethren are about to face a great period of persecution, a great war of the dragon against God's people. This is the central message of the Revelation the Lord has given me through his angel. This Revelation also promises us that the Lord is not ignorant of what is going on, that there is nothing that can be done against his sovereign rule or to thwart his plans. There is nothing that can be done against the reign of Jesus Christ, "the faithful witness, the firstborn of the dead, and the ruler of the kings of the earth" (1.8).

For many of us today in modern times, that seems to be something very difficult to understand. How can God allow his people or good people to be harmed and killed? How can he allow innocents to suffer because of evil individuals?

But Yann this world we live in is a fallen world. It is a world dominated by sin ever since the breaking of the relationship with God in the garden of Eden. Our Scripture's witness is that we human beings live in a world dominated by sin, and we ourselves so often speak and act as enemies of God. Why would those in your modern times not understand that?

That is a good question John and from my experience I believe our modern world and especially the world that has been the most influenced by the teachings of our Lord, does not believe in the seriousness of sin as the Scriptures teach. In fact, our modern world actually believes in the inherent goodness of man and at the same time in the unfairness of God.

Could it be that your modern world has been so shaped by the teachings of our Lord and the lives of those who serve him that they have forgotten what this world would be like without everything the Lord taught us?

How much goodness and respect of others would there be without the teachings of our Lord? For us living under the Roman emperors there is no doubt the world without Christ is a place of great darkness. There is no doubt about the meaning of Jesus' words as I quoted in my Gospel: "I am the light of the world. Whoever follows me will not walk in darkness but will have the light of life." (John 8.12). If there is any light shining in your modern world it is because of what the Lord Jesus has done and taught.

And as far as judging God as being unfair that is something that we cannot even consider seriously coming from human beings "dead in their trespasses and sins" and who follow "the prince of the power of the air, the spirit that is now at work in the sons of disobedience" (Ephesians 2.1,2). We know that we are from God, and the whole world lies in the power of the evil one. (1 John 5.19). And as I also wrote in my first epistle "**5** This is the message we have heard from him and proclaim to you, that God is light, and in him is no darkness at all." (1 John 1.5).

Tell me more about this promise of the Lord in the Revelation that he is coming soon?

Our God has come before, he is coming now, and he will be coming in the future. Thus, we find in our Scriptures that when there is a judgment of God on a people or on individuals it is often described as a "coming" of the Lord. When the Lord says he is coming "soon" he means quickly, speedily, and this is repeated seven times in the Revelation. (2.5,16; 3.11; 11.14; 22.7,12,20. A cognate word is also used in 1.1 and 22.6).

Could this simply mean that it is "quickly" in the eyes of God but not for men? That we look at time differently?

God looks at time differently than we do. However, if the Revelation was not warning of impending events, why would the Lord have repeated this throughout the visions for those who will soon face the harshest persecutions from the beast? When the Lord repeats to the Churches so often that he is "coming" unless they repent, does he not mean this for them, to bring them to repentance: " **4** But I have this against you, that you have abandoned the love you had at first. **5** Remember therefore from where you have fallen; repent and do the works you did at first. If not, I will come to you and remove your lampstand from its place, unless you repent." (2. 4,5; 2.15,16; 2.22,23; 3.3; 3.9; 3.20).

I remember now the very touching words of our Lord to the Church in Laodicea:

> "**19** Those whom I love, I reprove and discipline, so
> be zealous and repent. **20** Behold, I stand at the door
> and knock. If anyone hears my voice and opens the
> door, I will come in to him, and eat with him, and he
> with me." (3.19,20)

You see Yann, how in this case the "coming" of the Lord is not about his final coming but about his closeness and response to those who open the door of their hearts to his call. When the Lord promises the gift of the Holy Spirit to his apostles at the last supper he says, "I will not leave you as orphans; I will come to you." (John 14.18). This is not about his return in glory.

The Baptist came to prepare the "way" or coming of the Savior, the Christ as prophesied by Isaiah:

"**3**A voice cries:
'In the wilderness prepare the way of the Lord;
   make straight in the desert a highway for our God.
4 Every valley shall be lifted up,
   and every mountain and hill be made low;
the uneven ground shall become level,
   and the rough places a plain.
5 And the glory of the Lord shall be revealed,
   and all flesh shall see it together,
   for the mouth of the Lord has spoken.'"(Isaiah
7.3-5; Mark 1.1-8)

This coming of the Lord is also described as a coming of God's Kingdom among men: "Heal the sick who are there and tell them, 'The kingdom of God has come near to you.'" (Luke 10.9)

In many instances throughout our Scriptures the Lord "comes" to judge or deliver. The prophet Isaiah announced God's deliverance of his people through the Messiah:

"Behold, the Lord God comes with might,
   and his arm rules for him;
behold, his reward is with him,
   and his recompense before him."(Isaiah 7.10).

During his trial and in response to Caiphas, our Lord reminded us of the words from Daniel in his vision of the Son of Man and applied these words to himself:

"**63** But Jesus remained silent. And the high priest said
to him, 'I adjure you by the living God, tell us if you
are the Christ, the Son of God.' **64** Jesus said to
him, "You have said so. But I tell you, from now
on you will see the Son of Man seated at the right hand

of Power and coming on the clouds of
heaven.'" (Matthew 26.63,64).

The high priest is told that he himself will see this power of the
Lord seated at the right hand of God. This is the power of the
Lord as the Gospel spread from Jerusalem into the world and
as the chosen witnesses of his life and resurrection performed
great signs and wonders by the power of the Holy Spirit: "**2** For
since the message declared by angels proved to be reliable,
and every transgression or disobedience received a just ret-
ribution, **3** how shall we escape if we neglect such a great salvation? It was declared at first by the Lord, and it was attested
to us by those who heard, **4** while God also bore witness by
signs and wonders and various miracles and by gifts of the
Holy Spirit distributed according to his will." (Hebrews 2.2-4)

*I understand how the Lord coming quickly has to do in the
Revelation with the beast and these coming persecutions. But
in this case how could this be of any encouragement for the
saints who would live in the future, for us who are living over
two thousand years later?*
　　Remember that the dragon is still at war with God as you live
in the future. The Lord has not yet come for the final judgment
of the dragon, of Satan. This will only happen at the resurrection.

*What about these allies of the dragon? Yes, the beast and pros-
titute describing Rome the great city over the kings of the earth
has been vanquished. But does the dragon not continue to be at
war against the Christ and his followers? Does he not still
have allies to persecute God's faithful?*
　　This is true. But all the allies of Satan through time until
God's final judgment are not all described in the Revelation.

Why is that?

Well, if that were the case, we would have to carry around a much bigger book containing God's Word. Remember that even in my Gospel I wrote about all the many other things Jesus did and are not recorded in this Gospel and how "were every one of them to be written, I suppose that the world itself could not contain the books that would be written." (John 21.25).

I now remember how this point was brought up several times in our discussions. To go back to the invitation to the water of life, how are we to understand this invitation? What does it mean to come to the water of life and how does someone do that?

Jeremiah the prophet had prophesied to our people saying, "Though you wash with lye and use much soap, the stain of your guilt is still before me, declares the Lord God." (Jeremiah 2.22). The prophet Isaiah had called our people to repentance with these words:

> **"16** Wash yourselves; make yourselves clean;
>   remove the evil of your deeds from before my eyes;
> cease to do evil,
> **17**   learn to do good;
> seek justice,
>   correct oppression;
> bring justice to the fatherless,
>   plead the widow's cause."(Isaiah 1.16,17)

In the Revelation the water is viewed both to describe washing but also to describe satisfying thirst. These two ideas are found throughout our Scriptures and the teachings of our Lord. In the Revelation they are brought together at the end of the book the Lord says, "Blessed are those who wash their robes, so that they may have right to the tree of life and that they may enter the city by the gates" (22.14).

The white robes describe the purity of those who have received forgiveness, who have been washed by the blood of the lamb. I am reminded of the words of the Baptist following the baptism of Jesus: "Behold, the lamb of God who takes away the sin of the world!" (John 1.29). This is also what I have written in my first letter:

> "**2** My little children, I am writing these things to you so that you may not sin. But if anyone does sin, we have an advocate with the Father, Jesus Christ the righteous. **2** He is the propitiation for our sins, and not for ours only but also for the sins of the whole world." (1 John 2.1,2)

So, the ones who have washed their robes, who have received forgiveness through the sacrifice of the lamb, are also the ones who have come to the Lord thirsting for his forgiveness and for eternal life.

These words of the Revelation are similar to the words of Jesus to the Samaritan woman :

> "**13** 'Everyone who drinks of this water will be thirsty again, **14** but whoever drinks of the water that I will give him will never be thirsty again. The water that I will give him will become in him a spring of water welling up to eternal life.' **15** The woman said to him, 'Sir, give me this water, so that I will not be thirsty or have to come here to draw water.'" (John 4.13-15).

These words also bring us back to the Lord's sermon on the mount: "**6** Blessed are those who hunger and thirst for righteousness, for they shall be satisfied." (Matthew 5.6)

Did not the prophet Isaiah also speak this way somewhere?
  Yes, when he said:

> **55** "Come, everyone who thirsts,
>   come to the waters;
> and he who has no money,
>   come, buy and eat!
> Come, buy wine and milk
>   without money and without price."(Isaiah 55.1)

Why is this water called the water of life?
  Eternal life is offered by the Gospel of Jesus Christ to every man and woman who is dead through sin. Remember the words of Jesus to Nicodemus the ruler of the Jews:

> "**13** No one has ascended into heaven except he who descended from heaven, the Son of Man. **14** And as Moses lifted up the serpent in the wilderness, so must the Son of Man be lifted up, **15** that whoever believes in him may have eternal life. **16** For God so loved the world, that he gave his only Son, that whoever believes in him should not perish but have eternal life. **17** For God did not send his Son into the world to condemn the world, but in order that the world might be saved through him. **18** Whoever believes in him is not condemned, but whoever does not believe is condemned already, because he has not believed in the name of the only Son of God." (John 3.13-18)

APPENDIX

ROMAN EMPERORS

Octavian Augustus (emperor: 27 BC to AD 14). Augustus ushered in the Empire and the *Pax Romana* (or Augustan Age). Jesus was born under the rule of Augustus (Luke 2). Since the time of Augustus, the emperor had the title of *Imperator Caesar Divi Filius* which includes the title "son of God". This title was displaced on the coins used in the empire. Josephus writes about Caesar Augustus on many occasions, including his connections with Herod the Great and their relationship.

Tiberius (emperor: AD 14-37). Voted emperor by the Roman senate at the death of Augustus. Was emperor during the ministry, death and resurrection of Jesus (Luke 3). Was known as a "dark, reclusive and somber ruler" who never really desired to be emperor. A friend of Vespasian, Pline the Elder, the author of *Natural History*, described Tiberius as "the gloomiest of men". According to Josephus Tiberius "made death the penalty for the slightest offense" and people would be killed for even speaking ill of him. Josephus records that Tiberius Caesar was the emperor who placed Pontius Pilate as procurator over Judaea (Josephus *War of the Jews*, 2.9.2).

Caligula (emperor: AD 37-41). The name "Caligula" means "little boots". He was cruel and considered insane. The first emperor to rule with unlimited power. Writing about 70 years after Caligula's assassination, Suetonius in his "Life of the Twelves Caesars" recorded that Caligula "built out a part of the palace as far as the Forum and making the temple of Castor and Pollux its vestibule, he often took his place between the divine brethren, and exhibited himself there to be worshipped."

Claudius (emperor: AD 41-54). Under Claudius Rome conquered Britain (43 AD). Claudius appears twice in the Acts of the Apostles — once in 11.28, where we are told of a great famine which broke out in his reign, and again in 18. 2, where he is said to have "commanded all the Jews to leave Rome". After Claudius came Nero who was the adopted son of Agrippina the fourth wife of Claudius. Tradition has it that Agrippina murdered her husband Claudius using a poison mushroom.

Nero, also known as Lucius Domitius Ahenobarbus, (emperor: AD 37-68). At the age of 17 he became emperor at the death of his uncle Claudius, assassinated by Agrippina, his wife and mother of Nero. He was cruel, and lived in debauchery. There was a rumor that Nero was the one who a few years ago set Rome on fire which allowed him to build his *domus aurea* or golden palace. This rumor grew to the point that Nero pointed to Christians as the real authors of the fire. It was easy for him to convince the gentile population of the guilt of Christians who followed one who was executed as a criminal under the reign of Tiberius. The fire of AD 64 AD gave him the opportunity to persecute and kill many Christians, a growing population including many slaves but also nobles who would not render worship to the emperor. Nero is not mentioned by name but alluded to in Scripture especially in connection with the ministry of the apostle Paul (Acts 25.11; Philippians 1.12,13; 4.22). in AD 66 Nero sent Vespasian to Judaea to make war against the Jews.

THE YEAR OF CIVIL WAR: GALBA, OTHO, VITELLIUS (October, 68 – December 69 A.D.)

Galba (Ruled from October AD 68 to January AD 69). Also known as Servius Galba, he was the first emperor of what is known as "the year of the four emperors", a year of civil war (AD 69). At the suicide of Nero, Galba became ruler in Rome with the support of the Praetorian Guard. He was murdered a few months later by order of Otho who became emperor. *Otho*, also known as Marcus Otho Caesar Augustus, ruled over Rome for three months, from January 15, to April 14 of AD 69. A member of the noble Etruscan family, he helped Galba take over the rule and later ordered his assassination. After losing 40,000 men against Vitellius in the first battle of Bedriacum in northern Italy, he committed suicide. *Vitellius* (Ruled from April to July of AD 69). His troops and the senate proclaimed him emperor. The legions of Vespasian proclaimed him emperor and defeated the army of Vitellius during the second battle of Bedriacum. Vitellius was executed in Rome by Vespasian's soldiers on 20 December 69.

Vespasian (emperor: AD 69 - 79). December 21 of AD 69 Vespasian was declared emperor by the Senate. He founded the Flavian dynasty which lasted for 27 years. Vespasian had two sons, Titus and Domitian, both of whom became emperors. Vespasian launched a plan to rebuild Rome for which he inflated the currency of the sesterce and increased provincial taxation. According to Suetonius Vespasian was also the first emperor to establish a regular public salary for Latin and Greek teachers of rhetoric (Suetonius, *The Lives of the Caesars* "The Life of Vespasian"). He had besieged Jerusalem during the Jewish rebellion of AD 66 and subjugated Judaea. Vespasian initiated the construction of the Roman Colosseum. After he died in 79, he was succeeded by his eldest son Titus, becoming the first Roman emperor to be succeeded by his natural son.

Titus (emperor: AD 79-81). Titus, the older brother of Domitian, and the older son of the Emperor Vespasian. Josephus in his work "The War of the Jews" (Book 5) writes about the coming of Titus to besiege Jerusalem and of "the great extremity to which the Jews were reduced." Titus married Berenice the daughter of Herod Agrippa mentioned in Acts 12 (king of

Judea from AD 41 to 44). Titus could be the emperor mentioned in Revelation 17 who reigned "for a little while" after the ten years rule of Vespasian under whom John received the Revelation on Patmos (Revelation 17.10).

Domitian (emperor: AD 81-96). Younger son of Vespasian. He was considered as a "second Nero" concerning the persecution of Christians (Tertullian, Eusebius). After the suicide of Nero in AD 68, Galba, Otho and Vitellius were transitional rulers over a period of a few months (hardly emperors) in AD 69 which would make Domitian the emperor of Revelation chapter 17 described as "an eighth" but belonging to the seven: "This calls for a mind with wisdom: the seven heads are seven mountains on which the woman is seated; **10** they are also seven kings, five of whom have fallen, one is, the other has not yet come, and when he does come, he must remain only a little while. **11** As for the beast that was and is not, it is an eighth, but it belongs to the seven, and it goes to destruction." (Revelation 17.9-11). Revelation mentions five kings who have fallen (the first five emperors up to Nero) before the reign of "one who is" (Vespasian). After the death of Nero AD 69 we have in Roman history what is known as "the year of the four emperors" including Galba, Otho, Vitellius and Vespasian who started his rule that year. In this case the Revelation to John would have been given and written under the rule of Vespasian.

Roman Denarius depicting Vitellius

Fall of the Western Roman Empire

"In 376, unmanageable numbers of Goths and other non-Roman people, fleeing from the Huns, entered the Empire. In 395, after winning two destructive civil wars, Theodosius I died, leaving a collapsing field army, and the Empire, still plagued by Goths, divided between the warring ministers of his two incapable sons. Further barbarian groups crossed the Rhine and other frontiers and, like the Goths, were not exterminated, expelled or subjugated. The armed forces of the Western Empire became few and ineffective, and despite brief recoveries under able leaders, central rule was never effectively consolidated."[1]

MORE BACKGROUND ON REVELATION

At the end of the book the Lord Jesus gives an ominous warning to the readers:

> **"18** I warn everyone who hears the words of the
> prophecy of this book: if anyone adds to them, God
> will add to him the plagues described in this
> book, **19** and if anyone takes away from the words of
> the book of this prophecy, God will take away his
> share in the tree of life and in the holy city, which are
> described in this book." (22.19,20)

This warning is important since we know how many ideas have been claimed, preached and taught based on the book of Revelation.

So, how are we to understand this clear warning at the end of the Revelation given to us through John the apostle? How does

---

[1] https://en.wikipedia.org/wiki/Fall_of_the_Western_Roman_Empire

one add or take away from the words of this prophecy? How does one interpret imagery and symbols? This is puzzling since Revelation is packed with symbols and imagery.

One important response to this is to realize that **these symbols and this imagery are rooted in the Old Testament**, a foundational part of God's overall revelation. This means that our understanding of Jesus' revelation to John has to be informed by the language and meaning of the Old Testament. It has been estimated that there are 676 allusions or references to the Old Testament in the book of Revelation. This is especially true of the prophetical books such as Daniel and Ezekiel. The images, pictures and symbols God gave to John in this Revelation need to be understood primarily with an understanding of their biblical roots found in the Old Testament.

We should add that Revelation does not contradict what we learn from the Gospels or epistles of the New Testament; it is not some kind of new "gospel" and does not offer a different teaching from everything else in Scripture (see Paul's warning in Galatians 1.6-9). Thus, **a second way to look at this warning** is to be faithful to the Scriptures in fundamental doctrinal areas touched on in Revelation such as for example the nature of Jesus as the Son of God and Messiah; the importance of his death and resurrection; the meaning of his ascension and reign; the importance of his return and action in the final judgment; the injunctions given to Christians to live holy lives. These are all themes already developed in the New Testament (and for many in the Old Testament).

A third way to understand the warning of Revelation 22.19,20 is **to be careful not to understand literally what is meant as symbol or image**. This is true for example with numbers such as seven, twelve or one thousand. According to Merriam -Webster a symbol is "something that stands for or suggests something else by reason of relationship, association, convention, or accidental resemblance." A symbol is used for something which is already known, not something completely new or that we need to make up. The number **seven** signifies completeness already from the account of creation in Genesis 1 and 2 and throughout the Bible. We should not make up a meaning of that number that is not correlated elsewhere in Scripture just out of our imagination or by equating this biblical symbol with something we have seen somewhere else. The image of Satan as the "dragon" is quite easy to understand and also goes back to the "serpent" as a symbol of Satan and also rooted in the first chapters of Genesis.

This is also especially true with "apocalyptic" language borrowed from past judgments of God on oppressing nations such as Babylon. This language describing divine judgment against enemies of God is often taken literally by modern readers unacquainted with the figurative speech of ancient prophets, when the intention of the Scriptures is to remind the listeners and readers that God is the one and only God of creation who so often uses natural means to judge evil rulers and individuals, as in the plagues of Egypt (so for example in Revelation 6.12-16 the sixth seal is replete with allusions to past judgments of God over powerful nations and rulers who abused their power and mistreated God's people — see also Judges 5.1-4; Psalm 97; Nahum 1.1-5; Isaiah 13.13).

Additionally, we may also consider the importance in literature of what has been called "archetypes" many of which have developed from "apocalyptic" Jewish literature such as the first Book of Enoch (*BC* 200), the fourth Book of Ezra (BC 100), and the second and third Books of Baruch (*BC* 100). Archetypes can be described as "prototypes" or "blueprints" found in ancient and modern literature. Archetypes were fashioned over time often through an accumulation of a vast body of literature. They teach lessons that transcend time and space about behavior and human experience. The beasts found in the book of Daniel become archetypes of human empires that devour and destroy nations, such also as the beasts of the sea and the earth in the book of Revelation. What Rome as a beast ended up doing to God's people (Jews and Christians) can be understood as an archetype of what empires can do in all future ages to the people of God. The causes and reasons for these empires to exist and act the way they do does not fundamentally change with time.

The "dragon" or "serpent" is an archetype for Satan which dates back to the first book of the Bible, Genesis. From Genesis 3.15 we find the essential battle between the posterity of the woman and the posterity of the serpent, in other words the spiritual battle between human beings and Satan, God's adversary. This battle is found throughout Scripture but forms an essential background to the book of Revelation from the first to the last chapter. As noted by William Hendriksen in his commentary the book of Revelation can be divided into two main parts which are chapters 1 to 11 and chapters 12 to 22 with the introduction in chapter 12 to the evil work of the dragon in redemption history.

In the Revelation we are also reminded of **what Paul wrote in his letter to the Christians in Ephesus about their struggle with Satan:** "Finally, be strong in the Lord and in the strength of his might. **11** Put on the whole armor of God, that you may be able to stand against the schemes of the devil. **12** For we do not wrestle against flesh and blood, but against the rulers, against the authorities, against the cosmic powers over this present darkness, against the spiritual forces of evil in the heavenly places. **13** Therefore take up the whole armor of God, that you may be able to withstand in the evil day, and having done all, to stand firm." (Ephesians 6.10-13). The "allies of the dragon" (William Hendricksen) are worldly powers and rulers that rise up as "beasts" similar to the visions given to the prophet Daniel. The beasts are part of this archetype of a struggle between human beings and the serpent, between good and evil, between righteousness and sinfulness. Revelation does not refer specifically and by name to earthly governments and rulers (outside of allusions to the Roman empire and emperors) but the book presents to us a battle that has been going on since the birth of Jesus, his death on a roman cross, his resurrection and ascension until he returns in glory: "Behold, he is coming with the clouds, and every eye will see him, even those who pierced him, and all tribes of the earth will wail on account of him. Even so. Amen." (1.7) In this area the book of Revelation is not teaching or revealing anything knew since this is a constant theme throughout the Scriptures and especially the New Testament (see for example 1 Corinthians 15. 20-28).

The visions of the Revelation concern "**the things that must soon take place**" (1.1); "blessed are those who hear, and who keep what is written in it, **for the time is near**" (1.3). This idea is repeated twice in the last chapter: "These words are trustworthy and true. And the Lord, the God of the spirits of the prophets, has sent his angel to show his servants **what must soon take place**." (22.6) "And he said to me, 'Do not seal up the words of the prophecy of this book, **for the time is near**.'" (22.10). Note that John is told not to seal up the words of the prophecy because "the time is near".

This perspective must not be lost when reading Revelation. Does this mean that Revelation — a book destined first for the Christians living at the time of John and concerning events that would soon take place — has no message for Christians living throughout time and today? The answer is no because at the same time the book points out constantly what we might call the heavenly or eternal perspectives concerning "the things that must soon take place". This is not an idea original with the book of Revelation and in fact permeates the Old and New Testament Scriptures. In the book of Revelation as in all the books of the Bible the Lord helps us see things from the perspective of eternity, of heaven, of God. The one "who has freed us from our sins by his blood" is also the one who "is coming with the clouds, and every eye will see him, even those who pierced him, and all tribes of the earth will wail on account of him." (1.7). The Christians in Colossea had in fact "died" and their life was hidden with Christ in God"; When Christ would appear, they would "also appear with him in glory" (Colossians 3.1-4).

The heavenly perspective shown to John is one that is full of expectation and hope. However, the earthly perspective shown to John is one of pain and struggle. John himself is exiled on Patmos and writes to the churches in Asia as their "partner in the tribulation and the kingdom and the patient endurance that are in Jesus, was on the island called Patmos on account of the word of God and the testimony of Jesus." (1.9). John is a partner of these brethren because they too are enduring tribulation "on account of the word of God and the testimony of Jesus". Persecution is mentioned a number of times in connection with the life of the seven churches of Asia in chapters 2 and 3 (today's Turkey). The fifth seal opens with a vision "under the altar" of the "souls of those who had been slain for the word of God and for the witness they had borne." (6.9).

The tribulations these early Christians were enduring are directly connected to "the word of God" and "the testimony of Jesus". It was the preaching and teaching of the early Church that provoked the strong opposition of first century Roman culture. The word of God acted like a "sword" into the heart and life of the Roman pagan culture (see Hebrews 4.12) bringing some back to God through faith and repentance but also bringing others to reject these words and teaching contrary to everything they had grown up with, especially the significance of the gods they had grown up worshipping. "From his mouth comes a sharp sword with which to strike down the nations, and he will rule them with a rod of iron. He will tread the winepress of the fury of the wrath of God the Almighty. **16** On his robe and on his thigh, he has a name written, King of kings and Lord of lords." (19.15,16)

In these chapters of "dialogues with John" we are not trying to invent anything new or foreign to what so many great commentators have already said. If we had such dialogues for real, we would not be dealing with an apostle ignorant of the content of the Old Testament or ignorant of the content of the New Testament, including the epistles of Paul already recognized as authoritative by the time John receives the Revelation from the Lord. We would expect John to remind us of what the Lord had already done and said which confirms his revelation on Patmos; we would expect John to remind us of the prophets Daniel and Ezekiel or others.

The purpose of this book is simply to encourage readers to go back to the book of Revelation hopefully with a renewed interest and a better understanding of what Revelation meant to John and the early Christians and what it means for us today.

BABYLON AND ROME = LITERARY ARCHETYPES

Merriam-Webster: the original pattern or model of which all things of the same type are representations or copies, a prototype. **Cambridge Dictionary**: a typical example of something, or the original model of something from which others are copied. **Oxford Dictionary**: a very typical example of a certain person or thing. An original which has been imitated, a prototype…

RECOMMENDED READINGS

DAUNER, Max. *Commentaire sur l'Apocalypse de Jean.* Gigean, Editions Horizons Chrétiens, 1988. [Version électronique révisée, *Ils suivent l'agneau partout où il va (Commentaire sur l'Apocalypse de Saint Jean)*].

HENDRIKSEN, William. *More than Conquerors.* Grand Rapids, MI: Baker Books, 1940, 1967, 2015.

MC GUIGGAN, Jim. *The Book of Revelation.* Lubbock, TX: Sunset Institute Press, 1976, 2011

PRIGENT, Pierre. *L'Apocalypse de saint Jean*, Lausanne, Delachaux et Niestlé Éditeurs, 1981. (Commentaire du Nouveau Testament XIV).

ROBERTS, J.W. *The Revelation to John* (The Apocalypse), Austin, Sweet Publishing Company, 1974.

SUÉTONE. *Vie des douze Césars, tome III.* Traduit par AILLOUD, Henri, Paris, Société d'Éditions « Les Belles Lettres », 1964 (Collection des Universités de France).

SUMMERS, Ray. *Worthy is the Lamb*, Nashville, Broadman Press, 1951

About the Author

Yann Opsitch is an author, minister, teacher and evangelist to the nations. He is the director of l'Ecole du Maître (School of the Master), an online Bible training program for Christian leaders living in the French speaking world. Yann studied at the North Ireland Bible School, University of Geneva (Switzerland), Abilene Christian University, University of North Texas. He is the author of *Let Us Come Before His Presence: 365 Days to Learn, Meditate and Pray from the Psalms and the Sermon on the Mount.*

If you enjoyed this book, please consider leaving an online review. The author would appreciate reading your thoughts.

Visit the author's website at
https://yannopsitchauthor.com

You can also follow the author on social media at:
Instagram: @yannopsitch
Twitter: @opsitch
FaceBook: https://www.facebook.com/yannopsitch/
Linkedin: www.linkedin.com/in/yannopsitch

About the Publisher

Sulis International Press publishes select fiction and nonfiction in a variety of genres under four imprints: Riversong Books, Sulis Academic Press, Sulis Press, and Keledei Publications.

For more, visit the website at
https://sulisinternational.com

Subscribe to the newsletter at
https://sulisinternational.com/subscribe/

Follow on social media
https://www.facebook.com/SulisInternational
https://twitter.com/Sulis_Intl
https://www.pinterest.com/Sulis_Intl/
https://www.instagram.com/sulis_international/

www.ingramcontent.com/pod-product-compliance
Lightning Source LLC
Chambersburg PA
CBHW021616120626
46545CB00001B/256